Henry Parry Liddon, Edward Bouverie Pusey

On the clause and the Son

a letter to H.P. Liddon

Henry Parry Liddon, Edward Bouverie Pusey

On the clause and the Son
a letter to H.P. Liddon

ISBN/EAN: 9783744718059

Printed in Europe, USA, Canada, Australia, Japan

Cover: Foto ©ninafisch / pixelio.de

More available books at **www.hansebooks.com**

ON THE CLAUSE

"AND THE SON,"

IN REGARD TO THE EASTERN CHURCH
AND THE BONN CONFERENCE.

A LETTER

TO THE

REV. H. P. LIDDON, D.D.

IRELAND PROFESSOR OF EXEGESIS,
CANON OF S. PAUL'S.

BY THE

REV. E. B. PUSEY, D.D.

REGIUS PROFESSOR OF HEBREW, AND CANON OF CHRIST CHURCH.

LIBRARY ST. MARY'S COLLEGE

SOLD BY
JAMES PARKER & CO., OXFORD,
AND 377, STRAND, LONDON;
RIVINGTONS,
LONDON, OXFORD, AND CAMBRIDGE;
AND POTT, YOUNG & CO., NEW YORK.
1876.

[*All rights reserved.*]

PRINTED BY THE SOCIETY OF THE HOLY TRINITY,
HOLY ROOD, OXFORD.

CONTENTS.

Restoration of communion with the East free from our Western difficulties; would leave our devotions unchanged, and self-government, pp. 2, 3.
Hope of restored Communion with the Eastern Church expressed formerly, pp. 3-6.
ii. Denial of two Principles in the Godhead held to be sufficient explanation formerly, pp. 6, 7.
Cause of alienation of East and West; Crusades, Latin Empire and Patriarchate, pp. 8, 9.
Milman, p. 10.
Fleuri, p. 11.
Schism popularly excused by Greeks as self-defence, pp. 12, 13.
Attempts at re-union failed, because merely political, p. 13.
Terms accepted by Gregory X. repudiated by Nicolas III, pp. 14, 15.
Le Quien, p. 16.
Nechites on the Roman claims, p. 17.
Greek idea of hopelessness of union, p. 19.
Phranza on "the addition," Ib.
Inflated hopes of Greeks before Council of Florence, p. 20.
Objection to "the addition" made the battle-field by the Greeks pp. 20-23.
The insertion into the Creed said not to have been required of the Greeks, at Council of Florence, p. 24.
Limitation of titles given to the Pope, p. 25.
Privileges of Patriarch reserved, p. 26.
Dissatisfaction of the Pope at the refusal to elect the new Patriarch at Rome, p. 27.
Half of the Greek sees would have been permanently Latin, Ib.
Union rejected as a whole at once by Greeks, p. 28.
We have no claims to make, such as were rejected by them, p. 30.
iii. Bonn propositions too indistinct and incomplete to be brought before the English Convocation, p. 31.

iii. a. Ambiguity of the statement that "the addition of the *Filioque* to the Creed did not take place in an ecclesiastically regular manner," p. 33.

Mis-statements at Bonn, p. 34.

Creed never purposely interpolated, p. 35.

Circumstances of Council of Constantinople which retarded reception of the Council or its Creed, p. 36.

Neither received by General Council of Ephesus nor in Council of Constantinople under Flavian, nor at the Latrocinium, p. 38.

Its Creed not known to S. Cyril A.D. 429 or 430, p. 39.

Clause in it disputed at first by Egyptian Bishops at Chalcedon, p. 40.

Creed of the 318 (Nice) not superseded but confirmed by Council of Constantinople, p. 41.

Referred to as *the* authority by S. Greg. Naz., President of Council of Constantinople, Ib.

Not known in Lydia, at Council of Chalcedon, p. 42.

Creed of Constantinople received at Chalcedon as a second Creed, not as superseding that of Nice, Ib.

No regulation at the time as to its liturgical use, p. 43.

No need in the West *then* for either Creed, since its heresies were practical, not directly as to God. Apostles' Creed used, p. 44.

Reception of Council of Constantinople in West delayed by the rejection of its 3rd Canon, Ib.

Canons of Nice, rule of African and Spanish Churches, p. 45.

Local use of Creed of Constantinople once a year in a partly Greek population of France, Ib.

Nicene Creed first mentioned in Western Offices after 3rd Council of Toledo, p. 46.

Account of Council of Toledo A.D. 598, from its Acts, Ib.

Its entire loyalty to the Council of Constantinople; directed its Creed to be sung at the Mass in conformity to practice of the East [recently enforced by Justin the younger, *Addenda* p. 184.], p. 49.

"Procession of the Holy Ghost from the Father and the Son" already familiar to Spain from—

i. Rule of Catholic Faith framed against Priscillianism soon after 1st Council of Toledo A.D. 400, p. 50.

ii. Athanasian Creed. Internal evidence of its early date, p. 51.

Statements of "the Procession" in Latin fathers of 5th century, repetitions of that Creed, p. 52.

S. Paulinus, Prudentius, Ib.

Variations of S. Martin A.D. 375 and an Eucherius, p. 53.

Identity in Eucherius of Lyons, Ib.

S. Leo, Vigilius, S. Fulgentius, p. 54.

Gennadius, Julianus Pomerius, p. 56.

CONTENTS.

Paschasius, Boethius, Hormisdas, p. 57.
Ferrandus, p. 58.
Agnellus, S. Gregory of Tours, p. 59.
Formula of S. Gregory I, Ib.
Inference from this identity of statements.
S. Avitus, p. 60.
So Cæsarius of Arles, p. 61.
Use of Athanasian Creed in Breviaries, p. 62.
Canon of 6th century enjoins its being learned by heart, p. 63.
The *Filioque* then probably came into Latin copy of Nicene Creed unintentionally from the uniform Western use. Analogies in MSS. p. 64.
Devotional use of Constantinopolitan Creed in West began with this Council, and spread in the only form they knew, Ib.
The clause *Filioque*, once part of the Creed, could not be removed without risk to the faith, p. 65.
Leo III finally advised, not removal of the clause, but gradual disuse of the Creed, Ib.
Rome, the last in the West to use the Creed, p. 66.
No trace, that any Bishop of Rome ever formally received the Creed, p. 67.
Photius inferred once, that Pope Nicolas had inserted the *Filioque* in the Creed, three times denied it., Ib.
Baronius could not discover any Pope who received it, p. 68.
Cerularius asserted at first agreement of East and West, p. 69.
If the West had made any change for any needs of its own, this had been no more than Greeks did at Council of Constantinople for 70 years, p. 70.
Greeks could not condemn clause as heretical, without condemning their own forefathers, Theophylact, p. 72.
Basil Achridenus, Greeks under John Ducas &c. p. 73.
Proposition suggested to replace Bonn Prop. iv., p. 75.
Council of Ephesus only prohibited additions "contrary to the faith," Ib.
Occasion of its Canon, p. 76.
Prohibition of arbitrary acts of individuals, p. 77.
Related to *Nicene* Creed: had it prohibited *any* addition, would have condemned Creed of Constantinople, p. 78.
Canon abused by heretics to preclude their own condemnation, Ib.
Answer of Eulogius to Monophysites, p. 79.
S. Maximus in defending Council of Chalcedon, p. 80.
S. Cyril's explanation of his own Canon, p. 81.
Explanation by Council of Chalcedon, which renewed it, p. 83.
Canon forbade "*holding* any other faith;" had it meant to condemn all who held what it did not contain in its words, would have condemned every one, p. 85.

Wrong interpretation of Canon, ground of condemnation of S. Flavian by Robber-Council, pp. 86, 87.
The chiefs of Robber-Council condemned at Council of Chalcedon for that wrong judgement, p. 87.
The rest own themselves to have been wrong, p. 88.
Council of Chalcedon, which reenacted Canon, defended itself against this misinterpretation, p. 89.
S. Agatho, in VIth General Council condemning Monothelism, p. 90.
Second Council of Nice in like way, p. 91.
This instance, including the modern Greeks, adduced by Le Quien, p. 92.
Original objection not to the addition, but to the doctrine by the Monothelites, p. 93.
Their subterfuge answered by S. Maximus, p. 95.
iii. b. Doctrinal Propositions at Bonn: Dr. Döllinger embarrassed himself by confining himself to one later Greek writer, p. 96.
S. John Damascene, sound in substance, though rejecting language of earlier Greek fathers, Ib.
Apparent contradiction of the truth in one Bonn proposition on the Procession, p. 97.
Ambiguity, at best, of another Bonn proposition, p. 99.
Another Bonn proposition falls short of what S. John Dam. says in two places quoted, p. 100.
S. John Dam. believed the Eternal Procession of God the Holy Ghost *through* the Son, Ib.
This apparent from other sayings of S. John Dam. p. 101.
G. Scholarius, in his Eirenicon at Council of Florence, shewed that he understood the Latin doctrine, p. 102.
And that it was clear from the imputation of Photius, p. 103.
Latin doctrine carefully stated in definition at Florence, p. 104.
Proposition to anathematise the heresy imputed to it by Photius, p. 105.
Heresy imputed had been formally rejected by 2nd Council of Lyons, Ib.
Dr. Döllinger, Greek objections to our statement owing to misunderstanding our Latin term, pp. 106, 107.
Authorities in East and West,
S. Basil, p. 108.
S. Gregory of Nyssa, p. 109.
Origen, p. 111.
S. Dionysius Alex. p. 112.
S. Athanasius, p. 113.
S. Basil, p. 116.
S. Gregory of Nyssa, p. 117.
God the Holy Ghost said to have His Being "*from* the Son" by Didymus, p. 118.

To be "from the Father and the Son" by S. Epiphanius, p. 119.
"Out of" the Son, p. 121.
S. Basil, "has His Being from the Son," p. 122.
"From" in S. Cyril of Jerusalem, Ib.
Severian, Philo Carpathius, p. 123.
Anastasius Sinaita, Symeon Metaphrastes, p. 124.
Archbishop Theodore, how esteemed in the East, p. 125.
In Council of Hatfield before 6th General Council, p. 126.
S. Cyril of Alexandria, how esteemed in his own times, Ib.
Variety richness and precision of his declarations of the Procession from the Son, pp. 127-136.
Latin Fathers.
Both "from" and "through" in Tertullian, pp. 136, 137.
And S. Hilary, p. 138.
S. Ambrose, p. 141.
S. Augustine, p. 142.
S. Hilary, S. Ambrose, S. Augustine, S. Leo, recognised as authorities in other matters of faith by General Councils, p. 148.
Other Latin fathers before the 3rd Council of Toledo, given already, p. 149.
Latin fathers, as adduced in Council of Florence, owned by the dying Patriarch, Ib.
S. Augustine and S. Basil, a probable meeting-point, p. 150.
The far East. Council of Seleucia and Ctesiphon, p. 151.
Account of S. Maruthas in Greek history, Ib.
Testimony of Simeon A.D. 514, p. 152.
Council received by both Nestorians and Jacobites, and so prior to both, p. 153.
Nestorians. Elias of Damascus, IXth cent. Ib.
Ebedjesu inserts Canons in his collection, p. 154.
Jacobites. Bar-hebræus, history, Ib.
He inserts some of its canons in his collection, p. 155.
MS. containing the Council has nothing later than 7th. cent. Ib.
Impossibility of interpolation, p. 156.
Muratori deceived, for fear of being deceived, Ib.
Groundlessness of grounds of Bp. Hefele against it, p. 157.
Agreement of Syriac Scholars, Ib.
The Creed of Council of Seleucia, Ib.
Double Procession held of old by Nestorians, Ib.
Nestorians have it in their office, not in their Creed, p. 159.
Adam, Nestorian Archimandrite, Ib.
Jaballaha, Patriarch of the Chaldæans, p. 161.
Jacobites.
Liturgy called S. Xystus', Ib.
Renaudot, Ib.

Liturgy ascribed to S. Clement of Rome : Renaudot's remarks, p. 162.
Liturgies ascribed to S. Maruthas, Bar-salibi, S. Matthew shepherd, Ignatius of Antioch, p. 163.
Individuals. Xenaias of Mabug, Ib.
Dionysius iii, p. 164.
The Armenian Church.
Council of Shiragvan A.D. 862. Its character, p. 165.
It affirms the double Procession, p. 166.
Council, held A.D. 1342, mentioned ancient prayer used in the whole Church of the Armenians, confessing the Procession "from the Father and the Son," pp. 166, 167.
Armenians had their own special Creed framed for their own needs, not containing the Procession, and so they had not their then doctrine from Rome, pp. 167, 168.
They do not use the modern Greek phrase "proceedeth from the Father alone," p. 169.
They only deny that the Son is *the* Cause, Ib. and 170.
Limited object of this work, to remove prejudices, not to embrace the whole Theology of the Procession, pp. 170-172.
Some passages of Holy Scripture which imply the eternal Procession, pp. 172-174.
Our Lord referred the Procession of the Holy Ghost to the Father, as He did all else of His, having all things from Him, p. 174.
Evasion of language of old Greek fathers, who affirm the eternal Procession *through*, by some Greeks, p. 175.
The doctrine of a mere temporal Procession from the Son represents God other than He has revealed Himself, Ib.
God the Son and God the Holy Ghost would stand in the relation, denied by the fathers, analogous to that of brothers, p. 176.
Doctrine of In-existence of the Three Blessed Persons essential to the Unity of God, Ib.
Doctrine of In-existence as taught by S. Cyril, S. Basil, S. John Damascene, p. 177.
Alcuin, p. 178.
Western statement of the Procession "from the Father and the Son" has been a safeguard against heresy, p. 179.
Hopes for the future, p. 180.
Note I. Amendments suggested to some of the Bonn Propositions, p. 182.
Note II. Contemporary account of enforcement of rule, adopted in Council of Toledo, just before in the East, p. 184.
Note III. Corrections of some statements of Bishop Pearson on the insertion of the Filioque, p. 185.

A LETTER,

ERRATA.

CONTENTS, p. iv. *for* "Account of Council of Toledo, 598," *read* "589."
Page 62 line 6 from bottom, *for* "1600," *read* "about 1140."
— 103 — 35, *for* "believed," *read* "believe."
— 169 note q end : *for* "Mr Malan tells me that neither exists in any *known* writing of S. Gregory or of S. Eliseus," *read* "in any work of S. Gregory or of S. Eliseus *which he has*," for Mr. Malan tells me, "I have not all of them."

Conference, and how they could be modified, so that I could myself accept them.

This I do the more readily, because it was partly at my instance that you undertook that journey to Bonn, at much inconvenience, I believe, to yourself, and because I know that we are substantially of one mind on this subject, as on others.

I hope that I may do this less unsatisfactorily, if I embody in it, what I wrote, two years ago on this, the saddest of all our sad controversies. For it is, in the end, a controversy as to the Being of God, among those who really believe in God, who prize right and true belief in God above all things, who, each, doubt not that they have the right belief, and who *do* believe the same one with the other, if they could but look calmly at each other's mode of speech. It would be a happy employment of closing years of one's life here, in any degree to help our brethren in the Eastern Church to understand our Western language, and to induce some (especially our brethren in the United States) to pause in their eagerness to sacrifice our old expression of belief, under a mistaken idea that so they will promote unity.

1st. Plainly it is a duty to do what we can by way of explanation, which may any how tend to the healing of any of the breaches in the mystical Body of Christ. We know that we are all members of His great Family, although unhappily there is disunion among the members of that One Family. But the cause of this disunion does not lie with us. There is actually nothing on our side, to prevent any Greek Catholic from communicating with us, if the authorities of his own Church would permit it, nor are the members of the English Church in any way hindered from communicating in either a Greek or Roman Church, if the authorities of those Churches (or, in any case, of the latter) did not insist upon the renunciation of our Communion as a necessary condition thereto. I think that, if this had been attended to, some of those painful statements as to one aspect of the Greek Church, which we have heard of late, would perhaps have been spared. Those who made them, not knowing of the great work which the Russian Church has done of late years for the conversion of the heathen (far more than ourselves), have thought of the amount of the cultus of the B. V. among them. They have paralleled them with the Roman devotions, to which we have objected. But they have overlooked that, in regard to the Roman devotions, we stood on the defensive. Few probably would have thought it their business to question, what devotions were used in Spain or Italy. Our concern was, that they should not be forced upon us, as they would be, were our Bishops chosen for us by the Bishops of Rome. In the event of restored intercommunion with the East, there would be no interference with our self-government; and however we may and must deplore what is practically a system unknown to the Ancient Church, it is not our business to bring them back to their own earlier devotions, before they were interpolated by Peter Gnapheus [a], the heretical Patriarch of Antioch. Love and prayer are our only offices towards them. What is aimed at, is no change in either, except as, through increased love and intercourse, God the Holy Ghost may work any. The only primary effect would be, that the Orientals would admit to Communion such of our people as might be in the East, away from all other means of Communion; and *their* members would be allowed by their authorities to communicate with us, if they should be in the West, or in India or any other country where God has spread us abroad and their Church is not. Slight as this is, it would end the schism.

On this subject, perhaps, I may repeat what I said eleven years ago, embodying, in a book which has now seen its day, the thoughts of many past years.

"[b] The authorities of the great Russian Church

[a] Niceph. Callist. H. E. xv. 28. fin. T. ii. 634. See Rev. G. Williams on interpolation in Greek Liturgies in my Eirenicon P. II. pp. 425-427.   [b] Eirenicon P. I. pp. 263-266.

(we hear, as sounds floating on the breeze) look favourably on the wish for restored communion. Our position gives us an advantage towards her also; because, while we are wide-spread enough to be no object of contempt, there can be no dread on either side of any interference with the self-government of each, in the portion of God's heritage which, in His Providence, each occupies. We have no ground to fear in regard to her, lest she should force back upon us that vast practical system, still prevalent in the Western Church, which was one occasion, and is the justification, of our isolated condition. We had nothing to do with the great schism of the East and West. Convinced that (as the Council of Florence states,) the Greek and Latin fathers, though using different language, meant the same as to the Procession of God the Holy Ghost, we should have nothing to ask her,— except Communion. With regard to her too, we may have a Providential Office, that we too have received the *Filioque*, not by any act of our own, but as-circulated insensibly throughout the Latin Church; and while we could not part with what, through so many centuries, has been the expression of our common faith, we might still reject with Anathema the heresy which, since Photius, has been imputed to it, and which the Greek Church now seems, by an inveterate prejudice, to think to be involved in it. Yet it is plain that, long after the schism, her great writers and Bishops did not think so. Else they could not have proposed to the Latin Church, only to remove the word from the Creed, while continuing to teach or sing it elsewhere as they pleased. For had they thought the formula to contain heresy, this would have involved connivance in, and assent to, heresy. But if the objection lies only to the informality or mistake of altering the common Creed, this, it seems, was unintentional on the part of the Western Church; and *we* clearly had nothing to do with it. . . . We only ask to continue to use the formula, which without any act of our own, has been the expression of our faith immemorially. The Greeks, who value so much an inherited faith, could not, we trust, be insensible to the claim. If, on such terms and on such explanations of our belief as she may require and we could give, communion should be restored between us, a great step would have been gained towards the reunion of all Christendom."

It is not then on account of our recent disappointment at the decision of the Vatican Council, that our eyes have turned towards the East. We were taught by our public Prayers to pray for the whole Church; our good and devout Bishop Andrewes taught some of us to pray in his form for the Church, "c Œcumenical, Eastern, Western, our own," and " we hoped that the time was drawing on, when 'Eastern, Western, our own,' would melt, in visible communion too, into the one Œcumenical."

I wish, then, that the Bonn Conference had prepared for the restoration of intercommunion in a somewhat different way; but with its object I have entire sympathy. I have watched for many years for every crack in the ice which might be a symptom, that God would "d send forth His word and

c Eirenicon P. I. 275.   d Ps. cxlvii. 18.

melt them:" would "blow with His wind, and the waters flow."

ii. I much regret that your own proposal was not laid before the Orientals, that we, Westerns, while retaining for ourselves that form of expression, which we have had for 1000 years, rejected with abhorrence the imputation that we imagined that there could be "two Principles or Causes" within the Godhead. It is so monstrous, so opposed to the belief in the Unity of God, that I marvel how Photius could have mispersuaded any, that the Latins held it. However, the denial *does* meet the heresy, imputed by Photius to our Western confession: it was the explanation made by S. Maximus, when the same objection was made by the Monothelites[e]; that explanation of S. Maximus, together with passages of S. Cyril and S. Athanasius, changed John Veccus from an opponent to a defender of the Procession from the Son also[f]. When produced at Florence, it satisfied most of the Greeks. Even Mark of Ephesus said, "[g] whatever sayings of the Western saints agree with the epistle of S. Maximus to Marinus, I will receive as genuine, but all those which differ I will not receive." When the Emperor put the question, "If we should find the Latins accepting what S. Maximus wrote in his Epistle to Marinus, does it not seem to you good that we should be united through him? The Metropolitan of Russia [Isidore], the Bishop of Nice [Bessarion], and the great Protosyncellus [Gregory]

[e] S. Max. Ep. ad Marin. Opp. ii. 70.   [f] Pachymeres v. 16.
[g] in Syropulus Sect. viii. c. 2. p. 218. Syrop. adds, "This pleased the great Protosyncellus, and most, except some few."

agreed in this, and wished to persuade all to accept it. Only [Mark] of Ephesus and the metropolitan of Heraclea [Antony] and some few, dissented. For Mark said[h], 'that the Latins hold the contrary doctrine to what S. Maximus says. How then should we be united with them, when they only say in word that they accept what S. Maximus says, but by themselves hold the contrary and preach it in their Churches? First must they confess our doctrine clearly and unambiguously, and so we be united.'" Both parties were agreed that, if the Westerns did really hold what S. Maximus held, this would suffice. At the last, in the 23rd session, when the Epistle of S. Maximus was found and read, the author of the Greek Acts (probably Dorotheus of Mitylene[i]) says "This letter having been read, we, leaving what the Latins had written and all else, gave our minds to the Epistle of S. Maximus, and said, all of us together; 'if the Latins acquiesce in this Epistle, we, seeking nothing else, will be united with them.' The Emperor then pronounced, and the Synod gave sentence thereto, the patriarch agreeing therewith, and the Synod urged the Emperor to refer to the Pope and those with him, whether they accept the Epistle and confession of S. Maximus, and so to report to us[j]." Even lately, when the Archpriest Wassilief was so good as to

[h] Syrop. Sect. viii. 5. p. 222.
[i] Hefele remarks that, having named the Archbishops of Russia, Nice and Mitylene," the writer says, "we." He thought at one time, that he was probably Bessarion (Nice) but adds that "Frommann and others have found more probability for Archbishop Dorotheus of Mitylene." Concil-gesch. vii. 665.
[j] Sess. xxiii. fin. col. 385. Col.

come here and confer with us about the possibility of union, he was perfectly satisfied with our rejection of there being two Αἰτίαι in the Godhead.

Nor is the final failure of the Council of Florence to effect an union, any indication of the insufficiency either of this explanation, or of the fuller form adopted by that Council. The causes of that failure lay deeper. Every historian is agreed in this, that the Crusades hopelessly estranged East and West. A modern R. C. writer has expressed his belief that Constantinople was as much an object of the Crusades, as the Holy Land. Fleuri says that this was all along the impression of the Greeks. "[k] The Greeks always believed that the Latins had an eye to their empire, and what happened not 50 years after [the 2nd Crusade,] too well justified their suspicions.—The conquest of Constantinople brought about the loss of the Holy Land, and made the schism of the Greeks irreconcileable." The horrors of the 2nd capture of Constantinople A. D. 1204, might have been forgotten. It was more ominous for the future, that Innocent, although he strongly censures the capture of a Christian city by those vowed to the Crusade against the Saracens, and still more the atrocities committed[l], approved of the result[m], the establishment of the Latin empire at Constantinople, and a Latin Patriarchate, displacing the Greek. He congratulated the new Latin

[k] Sixième discours sur l' hist. Eccl. n. v. H. E. xviii. pp. xiv-xvi.
[l] "How shall the Greek Church return to ecclesiastical unity and respect for the Apostolic see, when they have beheld in the Latins only examples of wickedness and works of darkness, for which they might well abhor them worse than dogs?" &c. Epist. viii. 126. ap. Milman v. 351. [m] Innoc. Epp. L.7. ep. 153.

Emperor Baldwin, "on the marvellous work of God towards him, to the honour praise and glory of His own Name, to the honour and advancement of the Apostolic see, and the profit and exaltation of the Christian people [as if the Greeks were heathens] and praises his prudence, that thou ascribest little or nothing to thy power but all to God as the Author and to us." The Latin Patriarch of Constantinople complained in the Council of Lyons A. D. 1245, that he had scarcely 3 suffragans out of 30 which he had once had, and that the Greeks had been so successful in recovering their own empire; "ⁿ violently occupying the whole Roman empire up to the gates of Constantinople." The Council lamented that, notwithstanding the toils expenses labours and lamentable blood-shedding of Catholics, it was not rescued from the dominion of the adversaries and brought back to the unity of the Lord's body; it gave a subsidy for the support of the Latin empire, and the same indulgence was given to those who aided in its maintenance, as was given to those who joined the actual Crusade º. The Greek Christians were ranked as the Saracens. It was to be a sort of martyrdom to lose life in war with them. The Latin empire of Constantinople lasted only half a century. But the Greeks learned, that the acknowledgement of the authority of the Pope meant the suppression of their own hierarchy and of their own rites. What was left was tolerated only and removable at pleasure ᵖ.

ⁿ Matt. Paris Hist. Angl. A. 1215.
º Conc. Lugd. cap. 14. Conc. xiv. 57. Col.
ᵖ Innocent iii Ep. 10. ad Otton. Card. gives directions, which of a certain number may be allowed.

"ᑫThe establishment of Latin Christianity in the East was no less a foreign conquest" [than the empire], said one, who himself despised the Greeks. "It was not the conversion of the Greek Church to the Creed, the usages, the ritual, the Papal supremacy of the West: it was the foundation, the superinduction of a new Church, alien in language, in rites, in its clergy, which violently dispossessed the Greeks of their churches and monasteries, and appropriated them to their own uses. It was part of the original compact between the Venetians and the Franks, before the final attack on the city, that the churches of Constantinople should be equally divided between the two nations: the ecclesiastical property throughout the realm was to be divided, after providing for the maintenance of public worship according to the Latin form by a Latin clergy, exactly on the same terms as the rest of the conquered territory."—"ʳ No sooner was order restored, than the Franks and Venetians took possession of the churches as their own: the principal clergy had fled; the inferior seem to have been dismissed or even driven out, as if they had been Mohammedan Imaums: of provision for the worship of the Greeks according to their own ritual, in their own language, nothing is heard." This received some modification. But "ˢ this tardy and extorted toleration had probably no great effect in allaying the deepening estrangement of the two Churches."

Even when the Greek sees were left, Fleuri too observes that the Latin Bishoprics were unduly multiplied.

ᑫ Milman l. c. p. 349. ʳ Ib. p. 353. ˢ Ib. p. 366.

"†You have seen that, after the conquest of Antioch Jerusalem and other cities, Latin Patriarchs and Bishops were established there, and so again after the conquest of Constantinople. The difference of language and rites obliged the Latins to have their own clergy; but I do not see that it was well to be so eager, and so to multiply Bishops for the Latins, who were so few. Could not e. g. the Patriarch of Jerusalem have easily governed the Church of Bethlehem, only 2 leagues off? The Crusaders had come to the succour of the Christians of Syria Armenia and others, who all had their Bishops in long succession. Yet I see in our histories little mention of these poor Christians and their Bishops, save on occasion of their complaint against the Latins: so, under pretence of delivering them from the Moslems, they laid on them a new slavery.

"The first care of the Latin Bishops was to found well the temporalities of their Churches and to gain for them seignories cities and fortresses, as beyond seas, and they were no less careful to preserve them. Scarce were they established, when they had great differences with the Seignors, as the Patriarch of Jerusalem with the king for the domain of that city, and not less for the spiritual jurisdiction, among themselves or with the knights of the military orders, too jealous of their privileges. To settle all these differences, it was necessary to have recourse to Rome; whither the Patriarchs themselves were often obliged to go in person. What distraction for those prelates and what surplusage of business for the Pope! But what scan-

† Fleuri, l. c. n. ix. T. xviii. pp. xxi. xxii.

dal for the old Christians of the East and for the infidels!"

The Greek and the Latin clergy being thus side by side, the Latin powerful, the Greek poor and oppressed, the schism was, on the Greek side, almost a necessary condition of their existence. This is brought out [u] in a naive way by the Archpriest at Corfu, who with some other priests asked the Emperor on his return from Florence, how they were to act with the Latins. He answered, "as heretofore." They answered, "We have here no Bishop; but we examined those presented for the priesthood and received their testimonials and they were ordained by our Bishops. But the Latin Bishop here often desired to ordain them. But we said, that we cannot receive your ordination; and through the schism we warded off his request. But since the union has taken place, he will command us, that he should ordain. We do not wish this. What escape then have we?" The Emperor said, "We have accepted the union on these terms, that each side should retain the customs and order which it had before. If then the Latins should say any thing to you, say, that the union took place, so that we should have our customs and our order as before, and so they will not trouble you." But they rejoined, that "we are men enslaved to the Latins, and our word will not be received by them. For they will say, 'heretofore ye were separated. But now since you are united, and we are all alike, the ordinations too belong to us;' and they will not allow any one to go elsewhere to be ordained."

[u] Syropulus Sect. xi. c. 6.

"The Emperor decided, that the decree of union shall be transcribed, and ye shall have this to maintain what we say to you, and so they departed." The Emperor sailed the next morning, no one thinking of the transcribing of the decree.

At Methone, they complained of the completeness of "the defeat." "ᵛ If you had but corrected one of their errors; as that they should not celebrate on the same day three or four times on the same altar; or on the Nativity or Easter Day that one and the same priest should not celebrate from midnight till the fourth hour of the day, as often as he can; or any other wrong thing. If ye had corrected any thing which the Latins do, we could say to them, 'ye too were in error in this, and our's set you right.' But now we shall not be able to look them in the face. Ye have done us a great evil." In Eubœa the Greeks complained that the Latins now "ʷ could come indiscriminately from break of day and celebrate when they will in our churches."

The Councils for reunion failed, because they were merely political. Before the Council of Lyons, Michael Palæologus apprehended an invasion from Charles of Anjou, as the representative of the Latin Emperor of Constantinople, Baldwin. Before the Council of Florence, the Greek empire had shrunk before the Saracens within the walls of Constantinople. Palæologus was perhaps as sincere as people without strong principle are in emergencies, trying to gain now this side, now that, although inconsistently. To the Greek Bishops he minimised the three heads, to which he declared the Roman claims

ᵛ Syrop. xi. c. 8.   ʷ Ib. c. 9.

to be confined, "[x] the primacy, appeals" (which he represented as "empty, of necessity") "and the mention" of the Pope in the public prayers: he swore also "most awful oaths" that he "[y] neither thought of nor would take in hand the addition of one jot or tittle to the Creed." In the Council itself, the letter of the Eastern Bishops was conceived in the most general terms: those of the Emperor and of his son Andronicus accepted the faith, in the terms dictated by Clement IV, including "the Procession of the Holy Ghost from the Father and the Son," but requesting that "[z] our Church may say the Holy Creed, as it said it, before the schism unto this day; and that we may use the rites which we used before the schism, which rites are not opposed to the aforesaid faith nor the divine commands, nor to the Old and New Testament, nor to the doctrine of the holy General Councils, nor of the holy fathers received by the holy Councils, celebrated by the spiritual lordship of the Roman Church." These letters were formally acknowledged as a whole, by Gregory X[a], in separate Epistles to Palæologus and Andronicus and the Greek Bishops, and these were exhorted to bring back the people to unity. The requests of the Emperor were not formally noticed; still the whole letter was accepted and the union formed thereon. The *Te Deum* was sung, and the Greek Bishops had their seats assigned them.

[x] Pachymeres v. 18 p. 387. Bonn.   [y] Ib. c. 20. p. 395.
[z] Epist. Mich. Palæol. in Raynald A. 1274. xiii. xiv, and Conc. Lugd. ii. Conc. xiv. 507. Col.
[a] Greg. x. Epp. iii. 10, 11, 12 in Rayn. Ib. xix. xx.   Conc. Lugd. ii. Conc. xiv. 517.

Four years after, these requests of the Emperor were formally set aside by Nicolas III, as if they had never been entertained. Nicolas dissipated all hopes of any other relation of the Greek and Latin Churches, than that of absolute and complete submission. Their Patriarchs and Bishops were to promise absolute obedience to the Roman See; to bind themselves by oath to that obedience; their previous custom of not swearing was treated as usurpation against their superiors; it was peremptorily enjoined, as matter of necessity, that the Creed should be sung with the unexplained *Filioque;* only such rites were to be retained, as were approved by the Pope; it was to be suggested to them that the Roman Church wondered that their prelates and others had not petitioned to have the sentences against them in the time of the schism, relaxed, and themselves absolved from the irregularity of performing divine offices while lying under those censures, and that after this recognition of the primacy of the Roman Church and the promise of obedience, they had not asked for any provision, to confirm them in their offices[b]. Strange requisitions for the successors of S. Chrysostom and S. Basil!

No wonder, then, that the agreement made at the Council of Lyons was repudiated by those, for whom it was contracted. Even a Roman writer[c] says, "I will say, not without pain, that the union, made in the second synod of Lyons under the Emperor Michael Palæologus and the most holy Pope Gregory X., would perhaps have lasted, had not

[b] Instruction to legates in Raynald. A. 1278. vii-xi.
[c] Le Quien, Oriens Christ. T. i. p. 157.

certain of the points agreed on been derogated from, under Nicolas III., who succeeded him a few years after, at the instigation of Charles king of Sicily and some others. For whereas the fathers had allowed the Greeks to recite the holy Creed of Constantinople among themselves, without the insertion of the word *Filioque,* according to their ancient wont (as the Council of Florence again of its own accord allowed them), that other Pontiff who held the see of S. Peter, commanded them to recite that same word, as the Latins did. This so exasperated the minds of the Greeks against the Romans, that no way ever afterwards opened, whereby to bring them to restore sincere harmony with us."

Certainly, exasperation apart, it was a lesson not to place confidence in Latin Councils, if a concession made in a Council of 500 Bishops with the Pope, could be annihilated within 5 years by a Pope alone. And this injunction, if obeyed, must have been most bewildering. For the Greeks would have had abruptly, without preparation, to use to Almighty God a confession as to His Being, which, in the sense which they had been taught so long to attach to it, would involve, what the whole Church would rightly account to be heresy. Nicetas Bishop of Nicomedia, after acceding (according to the statement of Anselm of Havelberg A.D. 1245) to the expression of doctrine itself, said, "[d] Since these words, 'The Holy Spirit proceedeth

---

[d] Anselm. Havelberg. Diall. L. ii. c. 27. in Dachery Spicil. T. ii. p. 191. A Bp. Nechites was "one of 12 Didascaloi, to whom difficult questions were referred." The dialogues are given from memory. Ib. p. 163.

from the Son,' have not hitherto been publicly uttered in the Churches of the Greeks, they could not by any means be of a sudden publicly taught or written without some scandal of the people or of some less instructed." He thought that it might be effected through a General Council.

But the radical difference of the East and West was that, while the Greeks, like ourselves, would acknowledge a Primacy of the See of Rome, the See of Rome claimed ordinary and absolute jurisdiction; not a right of interference in any doubtful point, or of monition in any neglect or contradiction of the Canons, but an entire and irresponsible authority. Nechites states the Greek exceptions to the Roman claims.

" ᵉ The Roman Church, to which we do not deny the primacy among these sisters [the other Patriarchates] and to which, presiding in a general Council, we recognise the first place of honour to belong, has, for its loftiness, separated herself from us, when she assumed a Monarchy, not belonging to her office, and divided the Bishops and Churches of East and West, when the Empire was divided. If then she holds at any time a Council with Western Bishops without us, let those receive its decrees and observe them with due reverence, by whose advice she dictates what she judges ought to be dictated, and with whose assent those things are enacted which she judges ought to be enacted. But we, although in that same Catholic faith we do not disagree with the Roman Church, yet because we do not now hold Councils with her, how should we

ᵉ Dial. iii. 8. p. 196.

receive her decrees, which she made without our advice or knowledge?

"For if the Roman Pontiff, sitting on the lofty throne of his glory, wills to fulminate upon us and to project his mandates from on high, and to judge of us and our Churches, yea have empire over them, not with our advice but by his own will, according to his good-pleasure, what brotherhood, yea what fatherhood can this be?—Then might we really be called and be, true slaves and not sons of the Church. If this must needs be, and so heavy a yoke were to be placed on our necks, nothing would remain, but that the Roman Church alone would enjoy what liberty she willed, and enacting laws for all besides, be herself without law, no longer a loving mother of children, but the hard and imperious mistress of slaves."

Anselm, in answer, admitted the absoluteness of the authority, but averred that, if the Greeks knew how justly and tenderly it was used, they would, of their own accord, hurry to the obedience of the Roman Church[f].

The Council of Florence was from the first hopeless, not, as to the possibility of harmonising the two modes of expression as to the Procession of God the Holy Ghost, (which *were* harmonised so happily in its decree,) but because the Emperor miscalculated the temper of his own people, for whose reunion with the West (as a condition of Western succour of Constantinople against the Turks,) he had obtained that that Council should be held. His father, Manuel, dissembler as he was, better under-

[f] Dial. c. 9.

stood the temper of his subjects. "[g]My son, busy thyself about a Council and seek it, and especially when thou fearest the infidels, but never take in hand the holding it; for, as I see our people, they are not accordant to find any way or mean of union harmony peace and love and concord, except they are minded to bring back the Westerns, as we were from the beginning. But this is indeed impossible. For I almost fear lest the schism become even worse."

The early history of the Church had been so forgotten, and the idea of the *Filioque*, as an "addition," had been so ingrained into the Greek mind, that they conceived themselves as maintaining the old faith. "To me," says the historian Phranza[h], "my country's tradition of faith sufficeth; for I never heard from any of those parts, on the opposite side, that our's are ill, but rather that they are good and old, and theirs again good and not bad. To use a likeness, we have gone with certain on the spacious road in the midst of our city for a long time whereby to come to the Sancta Sophia: then, some time after, some have found another road leading, as they say, also thither; and they exhort me, 'Do you come this way which we have found; for although that, whereby you go, is good and old, and was known by us from the first and trodden with you, yet this too, which we have now found, is good.' But I, hearing from some that it is good, from some that it is not good, and there being this disharmony between us, why should I not say peace-

[g] Phranza ii. 13. who heard the speech, pp. 178, 179. Bonn.
[h] Phranza Ib. pp. 177, 178.

fully, 'go to the Sancta Sophia whence you will, and well be it; I again will go the way, which I for long time went with you also, and which you and your forefathers attested to be good, and went.'"

The argument is irrefragable, as against the attempt of Nicolas III. to force the "and the Son," upon the Greeks. Since the Greeks had ascribed heresy to the Latins herein, it was essential to union, that they should withdraw that charge thereon. On their doing this, each might, as Phranza, as a calm and candid Greek, suggested, have gone on their own way. "Would," he adds, "there might be an union of the Churches, though God deprived me of my eyes!" But he considered the Council of Florence as the beginning of the woes of his country. Its history, or any discussion of it, he professedly omits.

In regard to the Council itself the Greeks apparently had been inflated with hopes of an easy victory over the Latins; at least the Patriarch had used pompous language before the Council.

He had urged the Bishops to go to Italy, persuaded that the Latins would acknowledge their doctrine and form the union thereon, or any how they should proclaim the true doctrine, or be martyrs for it[1]. Neither party wished for any union, except upon their own terms; the Greeks to remove the *Filioque* from the Latin Creed; Rome, to obtain entire submission on the part of the Greeks. Mark of Ephesus, who was selected as the chief spokesman on the Greek side, kept, as long as it was allowed,

---

[1] Syrop. iii. 16. They were mocked for this on their return, "Had any one been tortured, scourged, imprisoned?" Ducas, xxxii. 31, p. 216.

from the real question. He held, or persuaded himself that he held, as Photius had taught the Greeks, that the Latin belief was heretical. But the one point which he put forward, was, that "the addition 'and the Son'" was forbidden. He desired then to make it a condition of union, that "the addition" should be struck out of the Creed. His object in this is best explained in his own words. They may be instructive to us. "[k] I sought that the addition should be cast out of the holy Creed, knowing that it was impossible that this should be done by the Latins. Or if it were done, it could have been done no otherwise, than by the Latins first condemning their own doctrine. For this it is, which is proclaimed by the addition in the Creed, which being cast out, the doctrine also would perish with it. And thus it would be well, if we were united in this manner. But if some should be left, who held this doctrine, this would be nothing compared to the whole fulness of the Church. For if the Church did not proclaim it through the Creed, it would gradually be extinguished from the minds of all: or with little trouble the Church would efface it."

The Patriarch, at one time, perhaps not seeing equally, with Mark, the result (that it must break up the conference) agreed, to require the removal of "the addition" from the Creed, as a previous condition to any further conference. "[l] Without this we will go no further. After its expulsion we will proceed to the examination of the doctrine, if ye will. But if ye cast not out 'the addition,' we

[k] Syrop. viii. 16. p. 241.   [l] Ib. vii. 6. p. 193.

will discuss nothing else, but will return home."
The Emperor annulled this with a strong hand, and
treated this counsel of theirs without his knowledge as an invasion of his prerogative [m]. Plainly it
would have annihilated the proposed object of the
Council, and would have cut off all hopes of Latin
succour to Constantinople. The Greeks felt, that
if they abandoned this, they were giving up what
they counted their strong ground; "where," they
say[n], "we have so much irrefragable strength," our
"[o] safest fortress," our "[p] strong, strongest point."
"This day" [of its decision], said one of much
account with them, "[q] brings either death or life."
The Greeks were much vexed[r]; "We know," said
one[s], when the union was spoken of as probable,
"that the Latins will not be persuaded to change
any doctrine which they have settled; ours must
have agreed to embrace theirs. Therefore they have
brought us here, to abandon our godly doctrine."
"We know," they all said to the Emperor[t], "that
the Latins will change nothing which they have
settled. *What* sort of union will it then be, the
Latins remaining as they are?" Mark wished to
collect the votes of the Greeks, before the discussion; but, at the instance of the Penitentiary and
Bessarion, was stopped by the Emperor.[u]. Gemistus, who confirmed the Patriarch in the rightness
of the Greek belief [v], thought it necessary to pro-

[m] Syrop. vii. 6. p. 194.   [n] Ib. 7. p. 195.   [o] Ib. 9. p. 199.
[p] Ib. 10. pp. 202, 203.   [q] Gemistus Ib. p. 200.
[r] Ib. 8. p. 204.   [s] The Bishop of Anchialus Ib. 13. p. 208.
[t] Ib. 14. p. 209. The patriarch, being ill, was absent.
[u] Ib. 210.   [v] Ib. vii. 8. p. 197.

ceed cautiously as to the arguments of the Latins, to hear them, and if they thought that they could overthrow them, well; if not, to seek in what other way they might gain what they wished[w]. And in the following conference, Mark twice or oftener remained silent[x], once the Emperor forbad his presence and that of the Bishop of Heraclea, as contentious speakers[y]. Mark openly declared all who believed the Procession from the Son to be heretical[z]. He threw out also vague suspicions of corruption of MSS. "[a]These things and the like being spoken, we rose, having effected nothing save division and schisms: for our synod was so small, that it was divided into two, and some following those opposed to the union, others, its adherents, were divided. And some of the rulers also dissuaded from the union and divided them."

The brother of the Emperor and Mark refused finally to sign the union. Syropulus relates that the Pope on hearing the refusal of Mark said; "Then we have effected nothing[b]."

Both the Patriarch and the Emperor had given their adhesion to the union on the condition "[c]that we should not put the Procession 'from the Father and the Son' into our Creed, but, observing all our customs, be so united with them." Syropulus relates that[d], on their return to Venice, Philip, the deacon, in the name of the Greeks, answered the enquiries of some English embassadors to the Pope; "Neither

[w] Ib. [x] Sess. xxii. col. 337, 341. [y] Sess. xxiii. p. 385.
[z] Sess. xxiv. p. 393. [a] Ib. [b] Syrop. x. 9.
[c] Sess. xxv. p. 492. The Emperor in the like terms, p. 493.
[d] Syrop. x. 18.

have we gone over to the doctrine of the Latins, nor the Latins to that of the Greeks, but the doctrines were examined on either side and found harmonious, and the doctrine appeared one and the same; wherefore it was arranged that each should retain the doctrine which it had hitherto, and we should be united; that it had been agreed that the Greeks should say the Creed without the addition [the *Filioque*]; the Latins with the addition; that the Greeks should celebrate with leavened bread, the Latins with unleavened; no Creed was inserted in the definition, not to exclude either form." If this were so, no terms could be fairer.

The Acts do not bear this out as to the Creed, except on a tacit understanding, such as that at Lyons. For it is formally stated that, with regard to the use of leavened or unleavened bread the priests should follow, each the use of his own Church, Eastern or Western; but with regard to the Creed, it is only said, just before, "[e] We define that the explanation of those words, *Filioque*, was lawfully and with reason added in the Creed, for the sake of declaring the truth, and under necessity then imminent;" which certainly seems to imply that the Creed should be so said.

Metrophanes however, when Patriarch, said in his encyclical letter [f], "You ought to know, that all our Ecclesiastical customs, both in the consecration of the holy Body of Christ and in other offices, and in the reading of the holy Creed, we retain as before, changing absolutely nothing."

[e] Definit. Conc. Flor. [f] published in Pitzipios l' Eglise Or. P. ii. p. 47, 48. from the Library of S. Mark. n. cvii. 5.

The Archbishops of Russia Nice and Mitylene, after allowing that there was no difficulty about the use of leavened or unleavened bread, or purgatory, and that as to the primacy, the Pope " could, after the union, have what appeared just," insisted peremptorily, " [g] As to the addition, we will never receive it, but we concede to you to have it in your Churches, yet not in those in the East: and we say, that you, under urgent necessity, expanded the Creed, and we do not call the 'from the Son' another faith or an addition, but pious and an explanation of our Creed; and both Creeds are pious and concordant, in the Roman Church, as you say it, and in the Eastern, as we say it, and thus let the union take place."

These Bishops were the warmest supporters of the union. They themselves disclaimed all authority to speak for the Eastern Synod. Their admissions were accepted: their requisition, that they should not use the "from the Son," unnoticed.

A Bishop from the Iberi [h] at the close of the conference is said to have shewn a tablet from the Patriarch of Antioch enjoining them [the embassadors] "not to agree to the addition or removal of a single jot or tittle."

The titles given to the Pope, in the definition, implied plenary authority, yet still in some way limited by the addition, "according as it is defined in the acts of the Œcumenical Synods and the sacred Canons." This is the more remarkable, because the words, originally proposed by the Latins,

[g] Conc. l. c. p. 508.
[h] Syrop. ix. 12. The other embassador was a secular prince.

"as Holy Scripture and the sayings of the saints define," were omitted. These had been excepted against by the Emperor, on the ground that any courteous language of a saint was not to be taken as constituting a prerogative of the see of Rome[i], and tacitly as excepting against the Roman interpretations of Holy Scripture. The term "[i] according to the sacred Canons" was suggested by the Greek Emperor. It is clear then, that the decisions of the Church as to the authority of the see of Rome, and not any inference from any words of Holy Scripture[k], were the grounds upon which the Greeks acknowledged that authority, and were consequently, in their minds, the limits of it.

The Greeks obtained also the insertion of the saving clause, "[l] saving all the privileges of the [Eastern] Patriarchs and their rights." The Greeks had insisted that, in the case of appeals, the power of the Pope should be limited to sending legates to hear the case upon the spot[m]. Finally this claim was dropped; on the other hand, the word "*all* the privileges," inserted by the Greeks, was excepted against by the Latins[n], on the ground that it might include all which they had used during the schism[o], but was at last conceded.

Yet, after every matter of faith had been agreed upon, the Pope said, "[p] I should not have known how to ask more from the Greeks, because what we have asked, we have had. After this matter of

[i] Sess. xxv. p. 517. Col.
[k] Hefele C. G. vii. 738. note.   [l] Def. Conc. Flor.
[m] Conc. l. c. p. 513.   [n] Ib. p. 521.   [o] Hef. p. 738.
[p] This which took place between the Pope and his Cardinals, is given only in the Latin of Justiniani Coll. xxii. col. 1179.

faith other things come to be done, and it is to be hoped that God will prosper us in other things also, and will unite us, as He has herein."

After the union had been signed, the Latins enquired about some of the Greek rites q, and the Archbishop of Mitylene having satisfied the Pope on all but two points, the annulling of marriage upon adultery, and that the Greeks ought not to leave "without a head;" nine days after the union, the Pope addressed the Eastern Archbishops who were still at Florence. "We, brethren, have been united in faith by the grace of God. Since then, by the secret judgements of Almighty God, I am become the head of your members, and any how I ought to advise and exhort what seems to be for the establishing of piety and of our Church, I have to say some things to you, as brethren, as members, as leaders of the Churches." The points were 1) the annulling of marriage [through adultery]; 2) the trial of Mark of Ephesus for holding aloof, "having been at a loss in the discussions and not being able to answer the questions of brother John" [de Turrecremata]; 3) the election of a Patriarch "here, where I am." To this last, on which most stress was laid, (as manifestly the appointment of Bessarion or Isidore, who had come to be on the Latin side, would have tended much to consolidate the Latin authority at Constantinople) the Greeks pleaded "the wont of their Church, that the patriarch

q This account is placed in the Greek immediately after the subscriptions; thanksgiving for the union having been made and "each of us having gone home." Conc. Flor. p. 533. Col. Justiniani questions this account (notæ ad Coll. xxii. 1196 Col.) but the Greek writer was present.

should be elected at Constantinople by our whole Eparchy." The Pope dismissed them with the threatening words, "If ye will not, I do what I ought to do, but ye will repent hereafter. 'If I had not spoken to you, ye should not have had sin, but now ye have no cloke.'" The Emperor warded off action. On the other hand the Greek Bishops could not obtain the withdrawal of the Latin Bishops who during the schism had been co-ordinated with the Greek Bishops, but only the concession, that if the Latin Bishop should die first, the See should remain with the Greeks permanently, whereas, if the Greek Bishop should die first, the See was to remain permanently Latin[r]. The result of this (supposing that the ages of the Greek and Roman Bishops had been, on the average, the same) would have been, that the half of the Greek Sees would on the next avoidance have become permanently Latin.

The Emperor's father had however too well estimated the result of an attempt at union, that the rent would become worse[s]. Monks and nuns[t], the religious as well as the irreligious, were against the union. Chiefly and rightly, it was the change in the language of faith. Why (as Phranza expressed it) should they change the old ways for what was to them new? Their objections were contained in the one word "latinise[u]." Externals were a sym-

[r] Syrop. x. 14.
[s] See ab. pp. 20, 21. [t] Ducas c. 36 p. 254. c. 37. 269. Bonn.
[u] "I would rather die than latinise." Dositheus Conc. Flor. Sess. xxv. init. "embracing latinism" Syrop. p. 337. "Thou hast latinised," Ib. "thou hast mingled and gone with the latinisers, before the latin-minded Patriarch" Ib. "agreeing with latinising."

bol of the whole: "we are become Azymites[v]," was a cry as much as "we have betrayed the faith," because it belonged to the same whole. Miserable as the violence of feeling was, it was not to be expected that the whole Greek Church should at once without argument, without teaching, without time, recognize that to be truth, which for centuries they had been taught to be heresy. And so the Churches were almost deserted, when any "latiniser" celebrated [w]. The Church of S. Sophia remained empty, from the time when the union took place in it [x]. The Emperor sought to induce them to allow the name of the Pope to be read in the diptychs, the decree of union being represented as "obsolete [y]." They would not recite the name of a "heretic." Even the Emperor's name was passed over in the diptychs [z]. The mild measures of the Emperor were useless; the severe measures ascribed to Metrophanes, the Unionist Patriarch, were fatal. The three other Patriarchs deposed those whom Metrophanes had made Bishops in place of the anti-unionists: they repudiated the union, the method of which they say Eugenius had not explained to them, but simply and peremptorily required their consent to it, and to place his name on the diptychs; and they threatened the Emperor with excommuni-

Ib. p. 235. "those who affected latinism." Ib. 255. add p. 331.

[v] "We have become Azymites." Ducas c. 32. p. 216 ed. Bonn. "far from us be the worship of the Azymites" (populace). Id. c. 36. p. 255. "let us see if God will remove this enemy who is against us, and then you shall see whether we unite with the Azymites [unionists to schismatics]." Ib. p. 256.

[w] Syrop. xii. 1. [x] Ducas c. 37. p. 263.
[y] Syrop. xii. 8. p. 343. [z] Id. 2.

cation, if he enforced the union [a]. Isidore, Archbishop of Kiew, who was sent with legatine authority to carry out the union in Russia, was imprisoned, but escaped [b].

And so this last attempt at the re-union of East and West expired, because too much was asked, and time was not allowed, in which the Greeks at home could be brought to see, that our Western form was that of some of the greatest of their own fathers, and did not contain the heresy imputed to it. The Westerns would not succour Constantinople, unless the union was completed. Constantinople was allowed to fall into the hands of the Turks, and East and West have remained permanently disunited.

I have dwelt the longer and the more in detail on these fruitless negotiations, as shewing that the real matter at issue was not simply the great doctrine which was put forward, but the political and ecclesiastical relation of the two great Communions. Rome attempted too much and lost all. We have nothing to ask, but that communion should not be denied to our members in the East, because we express our faith in the same language, as did some of their greatest fathers. We should come indeed with cleaner hands, had not earthly politics and the interests of our commerce thrown our country into war with Russia, in union with France and " our old and faithful ally, the Turk," as he was then called. Yet, miserable as that war was, and much as many of us at the time lamented it, as a war of Christians with Christians in behalf of that op-

[a] Allatius (de perp. consens. iii. 4.) printed the letters.
[b] Rayn. A. 1439. xi.

pressive Anti-Christian power, with whose deeds of ruthless violation of everything sacred to humanity Europe has been ringing, Russia perhaps will also bethink herself, that her motives were not altogether free from human alloy, and that thoughts of her own aggrandisement mingled at least with those of the liberation of Christians, so brutally oppressed.

iii. Of the resolutions adopted by the Bonn Conference, so long as they were only resolutions of that Conference, I had no occasion to speak. I was surprised at the jubilee of joy, with which they were received by the Church-papers and many Churchmen. For with the one exception of the general acceptance of "the doctrine of the Holy Ghost, as it is set forth by the Fathers of the undivided Church," there was nothing to protect or explain our Western Confession, which, if the words were taken strictly, two of those resolutions seem to me to contradict, and the introduction whereof into the Creed they apparently condemned. I feared, that they would only prepare the way for a demand on the part of the Greeks, that, if any Westerns wished to enter into communion with them, they should abandon the *Filioque*.

But there was no occasion for me to express any opinion about them. It would be proved, on the renewal of the Conference in the course of this present year, whether the Easterns would be instructed by their authorities at home to make any such demand, or whether they could really carry out the proposition, to which after some hesitation they had acceded; "We acknowledge on all sides the representation of the doctrine of the Holy

Ghost, as it is set forth by the Fathers of the undivided Church." If they could do this without reserve, our Confession would be safe. For, notoriously, the Procession of the Holy Ghost from the Father and the Son together, as being One, has been the mode in which, from S. Augustine's time, the Western Church has uniformly confessed its faith. The Greeks could not then, while acknowledging the Fathers of the undivided Church, ask us to abandon what has been in the West nearly the exclusive expression of our Faith from the earliest times.

It was not for me to damp the hopes of any by my misgivings. I feared that those at Bonn, in attempting their work of love, had laid a snare for their own feet, and had made admissions, from which it would be difficult to escape. But I always hope; and so I trusted that God would make a way to escape.

But the aspect of things was changed, when the committee of the Eastern Church Association began canvassing for signatures to a declaration, setting forth that those who signed it believed those propositions to be true, and praying the two Convocations to consider them with a view to promote a closer intercommunion (at present there is none) with the Orthodox Churches of the East. In this you had no share. I could not doubt that it was unwise and premature to bring the matter, in this inchoate and imperfect state, before our Convocations at all. We, Englishmen, always wish to know, whither we are going; what are the further bearings of any thing which we are asked to do;

what it will involve. I dreaded the discussion which would follow. I thought it wrong that the Church of England should be asked to commit itself to these propositions, whose bearings no one, even of those present at Bonn, knew; whether the authorities in Russia or at Constantinople would approve of them, or in what sense they would understand them. The doctrinal propositions were taken from a writer, who, although he held the same faith with us, formally rejected our language, whereas (as I have already observed) there was not a syllable in defence or explanation of that language. The whole seemed to me, not in a state, upon which any opinion could be asked of a representative body.

iii. a. To enter, as you wish, into detail: The 2nd preliminary proposition stands, "We agree together in acknowledging that the addition of the *Filioque* to the Creed did not take place in an ecclesiastically regular manner."

If this means, that it was not added by a General Council, and that "the acceptance of it could not be required of the Orientals," since it did not proceed from such a Council, it would be a truism. But it was not so understood, either in the Conference or by English members since. And a truism could not be put forth as the basis of an Eirenicon. For it clears up nothing. It would have been ludicrous, formally to enunciate, what every one knows, that the addition was not made by a General Council. Dr. Döllinger's statements were wholly different.

Dr. Döllinger stated that "[c] the *Filioque* was in

[c] Dr. Döllinger, Bonn Conf. p. 19.

the West arbitrarily and unlawfully added to the Creed:" "ᵈLast year we admitted that the *Filioque* was an illegal addition to the Creed, and that the acceptance of it could not be required of the Orientals." [Plainly it could not be required of *them*. The question is, not whether *we* should require them to receive the *Filioque;* but whether *they* would require of us to abandon it.] He said that in so doing, "a fault had been committed;" he regarded that resolution as "an open admission of that fault," and that the 2nd Article merely "ᵉ rectified, *as far as lies in our power*, an old wrong."

This imputation of "fault" gave a colour to the proceedings at Bonn, and threatens for the future. Bishop Reinkens told the Conference that "ᶠin the Western Church, *by the command of an Emperor*, the addition of the *Filioque* was illegally made." This was plainly contrary to the fact. "ᶠThis illegality we have now acknowledged, and thus this addition is removed from its place as a dogma, and the controversy ought to be at an end." In other words, it is no longer matter of faith. Professor Damalas of Athens was not slow to see the advantage, which the admission gave to the Eastern claim to expel this truth from our Western Creed.

"ᵍUp to the present time, the Westerns retain the *Filioque* in the Symbolum, although they acknowledge that it gained admission there as dogma in an illegitimate and, so to speak, not Old Catholic way: consequently, the necessary preliminaries for further examination and discussion are wanting, if

ᵈ Bonn Conf. p. 35. ᵉ Ib. p. 91.
ᶠ Ib. p. 57. ᵍ Ib. p. 63.

you do not remove the *Filioque* from the Symbolum
in accordance with your admission."

The misstatements on this subject have been so
grave, that it may not be without its use to go back
to the earliest history of the Creed. People speak
fluently of "interpolations" and the like. It seems
to me probable, that the Spanish Church had not
the Creed at all, until the date when they are said
to have interpolated it. The Creed itself was not
received as a Creed of the Church at all, until the
Council of Chalcedon A.D. 451. But Spain was at
this time under its Arian invaders and masters.

The following picture is given of its condition.
' [h] Spain was already nearly dissevered from the
Empire of Rome. It had been overrun, it was in
great part occupied, by Teutonic conquerors, Sue-
vians, Goths and Vandals, all of whom, as far as
they were Christians, adhered to the Arianism, to
which they had been converted by their first Apostles. The land groaned under the oppression of
foreign rulers, the orthodox Church under the superiority of Arian sovereigns."

Accustomed, as we are, to the devotional use of
the Nicene Creed, as part of our religious life and
the informer of our faith, it does not occur to us to
think, that the Spanish Church, or the Latin Church
generally, could have been unfamiliar with it.

Yet the unhappy circumstances, under which the
Council of Constantinople was convened, seem to
have retarded the reception even of its Creed. It
was a Greek Council, assembled by the Emperor
Theodosius, to stem Arianism, and if possible, win

[h] Milman Latin Christianity, i. 250.

the Macedonians to the faith. The heresies being almost exclusively Eastern, Theodosius "[i]assembled only the Bishops of his own kingdom to Constantinople." The only exception was Ascholius of Thessalonica, who came only as the spiritual father of Theodosius, having recently baptised him, when sick[k]. The unhappy intrusion of Paulinus by Lucifer into the see of Antioch, then occupied by the great S. Meletius, and his recognition by Rome, had alienated the Greeks from Rome. S. Meletius was out of communion with Rome, when he presided over the Council of Constantinople[l]. Even S. Basil had complained of the "[m]Western superciliousness."

After the death of S. Meletius, Pope Damasus dissuaded from the election of S. Gregory of Nazianzus, whom, in ignorance, he depreciated; and both he and S. Ambrose were deceived by Maximus the Cynic, (who had procured a private consecration to the see of Constantinople under pretence of letters obtained from Peter the previous Patriarch, before his decease,) and received him into their communion. The Westerns, including even S. Ambrose, acknowledged Maximus as Patriarch. The Bishops of Italy also excepted against the consecration of Nectarius, the deposition of Maximus by the Council of Constantinople, and the election of Flavian to the see of Antioch, during the lifetime of Paulinus, to which they alleged Nectarius to be a party; and two Councils, the one of Aquileia, the other, of Italy, begged Theodosius to interfere, by restoring

[i] Theod. H. E. v. 7.   [k] Socr. v. 6.
[l] S. Greg. Naz. de vita sua 1612. See Pusey's Councils p. 306.
[m] Ep. 239. Euseb.

Maximus to the see of Constantinople, or that a Council of Eastern and Italian Bishops at Rome should decide between the claims of Maximus and Nectarius. Else, that the communion of East and West could not continue [n]. The Eastern Bishops again assembled, declined to come to a Synod at Rome [o], and justified their proceedings [p]. The schism was not healed during the Episcopate of Damasus, Siricius, or Anastasius. Rome and Egypt remained unreconciled to Flavian, during the life not only of Paulinus but of Evagrius, whom he had made his successor, until, after 17 years, peace was restored when Innocent I. was Bishop of Rome, and Theophilus, of Alexandria [q].

One result of this state of confusion was the long neglect of the Creed, as enlarged by the Council, whose own proceedings were so called in question. At the third general Council, the Creed set forth by the 318 Bishops assembled at Nice was formally recited, as the touchstone of truth; S. Cyril's Epistle to Nestorius was also read. The Bishops in succession pronounced, in different terms, that the Epistle of Cyril was conformable to that faith [r], and, after Nestorius' answer had been read, pronounced again, one by one, that it was at variance with that faith [s].

Of the Council and Creed of Constantinople not a word is said.

It was again the proper Nicene Creed, which in the 6th session was read and inserted in the Acts [t],

[n] Ep. 2 Conc. Aquil. ad Theodos. Imp. Ep. 2 Conc. Ital. ad Theod. Concil. ii. 1185 and 1193. Col.   [o] Theod. H. E. v. 8.
[p] Ep. Synod. Damaso Ambr. &c. Ib. v. 9.
[q] Theod. H. E. v. 23.   [r] Conc. Eph. Act. 1. Conc. T. iii. 1008 sqq.   [s] Ib. p. 1037 sqq.   [t] Ib. Act. vi. p. 1201.

and to it alone, the so-often misquoted rule against using any Creed contradictory to this Creed on receiving heretics returning to the Church, relates[u].

In the Council of Constantinople under Flavian, (whose Acts were read in the Robber-Council of Ephesus and in that of Chalcedon) Eusebius of Dorylæum, the accuser of Eutyches, established his orthodoxy by the statement, that he "[v] abode by the faith of the 318 holy fathers assembled at Nice, and all which was done by the holy and great Council in the metropolis of the Ephesians, and what the blessed Cyril, Bishop of Alexandria, thought and set forth," omitting altogether the Council of Constantinople and its additions to the Creed of Nicæa.

In the Robber-Council, Bishop Julian, S. Leo's legate, excused S. Leo's absence on the ground of precedent, that "[w] neither at Nice, nor in the holy Synod of Ephesus, nor in any such holy Council, was the Pope of that most holy throne present; whence, following this custom, he has sent us." The Council of Constantinople, even if alluded to, is not named.

There was no reason, why Eutyches or Dioscorus should slight the Council of Constantinople; for its additions were not directed against their errors. Their exceptions were against what Flavian ruled, what the Council of Chalcedon subsequently affirmed. But in respect of the past Councils they do no other than the Roman Legates or Eusebius. Eutyches says under his " confession of faith, '[x] I am

[u] Ib. 1220.   [v] Act. Constantinop. in Conc. Eph. sub Dioscoro relecta Conc. Chalc. Act. 1. Conc. iv. 932.
[w] Gesta Ephesi in Conc. Chalc. Conc. iv. p. 896. Col.
[x] Ib. p. 924.

minded as the holy fathers, assembled at Nice, delivered to us to believe, which also the holy fathers at Ephesus *at the second Council* confirmed, and if any one dogmatizes beside this faith, I anathematise him according to their definition.'" And just before, "ʸAnd when I was commanded to express my own confession of faith and said, that I was minded as the 318 holy fathers at Nice decreed, and the holy Synod at Ephesus confirmed, he [Flavian] enquired of me other things, beside what was set forth both in the Council of Nice and at Ephesus. But I, fearing to transgress the definition made by the holy Synod gathered here before by the will of God &c."

And so, in a long series, the Bishops of the Robber-Council ground their acquittal of Eutyches, in varied words, on his agreement with the 318 holy fathers assembled at Nice and the former Council assembled in this metropolis at Ephesus[z], which, Dioscorus said, "[a] Though they are called two Councils, yet accord to one faith." "The holy Synod said, 'The fathers defined all, omitting nothing. Anathema to him who transgresses these things. No one adds; no one subtracts.'"

The reconciliation of Constantinople with Egypt having only been at the beginning of the 5th century, it is the less surprising, although it furnishes a remarkable trait in the picture of those times, that not these only, but S. Cyril of Alexandria in 429 or 430, should not have been acquainted with the Creed of Constantinople.

Nestorius, as Patriarch of Constantinople, quoted the Nicene Creed, with some additions of the Coun-

[y] Ib. p. 920.   [z] p. 1100. sqq. Col.   [a] p. 908. Col.

cil of Constantinople (as we do now) under the title of "the Nicene Creed." The Creed, as drawn up at Nicæa, had only the words, "Who, for us men and for our salvation, came down and was incarnate." The fathers at Constantinople added, "from heaven," after "came down;" and after "incarnate," "of the Holy Ghost and the Virgin Mary." Nestorius quoted the Nicene Creed with the additions of that of Constantinople, "[b] came down from heaven for us, and was incarnate of the Holy Ghost." S. Cyril recites the actual Creed of Nicæa itself, and then asks Nestorius, to "'[c] say, where they laid down as to the Son, that He 'was incarnate of the Holy Ghost and the Virgin Mary'" which he treats, as "an innovation of this man." This, of course, he could not have done, had he known that the words were added in the Council of Constantinople.

Two years after the Robber-Council, at the Council of Chalcedon, which subsequently received the Creed, the Egyptian Bishops present formally rejected its additions. The following scene is recorded in the Acts:

> "Diogenes, Bishop of Cyzicus, said, 'The holy fathers who met at Nice said that HE WAS INCARNATE. But the holy fathers explained the words, HE WAS INCARNATE which the holy fathers said, by saying, OF THE HOLY GHOST AND THE VIRGIN MARY. Upon this the Egyptians and the most reverend Bishops with them, shouted out, 'No one receiveth addition; no one, diminution. Let the things at Nice prevail.' The Eastern and most reverend Bishops with them cried out, 'This said Eutyches.' The Egyptians,

[b] Adv. Nest. i. 7. Opp. T. vi. p. 22. Aub., p. 82. ed. Oxon.
[c] Ib. c. 8. p. 25. Aub., 85. Oxon. This was pointed out to me by the Editor, my son.

and the most reverend Bishops with them, said, 'No one receiveth addition; let the things of the fathers prevail, let the things of the Holy Spirit prevail! The orthodox king enjoins this.'"

It is indeed obvious that the Council of Constantinople did not mean to displace or replace the Creed of Nicæa. For the first canon of the Council of Constantinople provides for the retention of the Nicene Creed. It is,

> "That the faith of the 318 holy fathers, who met at Nice be not set aside, but remain authoritative, and that every heresy be anathematized."

S. Gregory of Nazianzus, (who, although he had resigned the See of Constantinople which had been forced upon him, and therewith the Presidency of the Council, yet signed its Acts as Bishop of Nazianzus) referred to the Creed of Nice as *the* authority. He writes thus to Cledonius who asked him in the name of many others:

> "[d] Since many, coming to your reverence, seek full assurance as to faith, and so you have lovingly asked us for a brief definition and rule of our thought, we have therefore written to your reverence, (which indeed you knew, before we wrote) that we never have preferred, nor can prefer any thing to the faith at Nice, that of the Holy fathers who met there for the destruction of the Arian heresy, but we, by the help of God are and will be of that faith, completing in addition, what they said inadequately of the Holy Ghost (because that enquiry had not yet been mooted) that we must know that the Father and the Son and the Holy Ghost are of one Godhead, knowing the Spirit to be God."

Charisius, a Presbyter of Philadelphia in Lydia,

[d] Epist. 102 (ad Cledon. 2.) init. Opp. ii. 93, 94. Bcn.

making complaint to the Council of Ephesus against some Nestorian emissaries from Constantinople, and so having to establish his own orthodoxy, sent in, with his signature, not the Creed of Constantinople, but, what must have been a local Creed [e], agreeing in substance with it, mostly in words, save that it affirms " the Spirit of truth, the Paraclete, to be " consubstantial with the Father and the Son," and does not mention His Procession at all. The Creed of Constantinople had not then penetrated to Lydia.

The Creed of Constantinople accordingly was first received, not as replacing the Creed of Nice, but in addition to it, in the Council of Chalcedon :

> "[f] We, guarding the order and all the formulæ concerning the faith, define, that before the holy Synod formerly held at Ephesus, of which the presidents were Celestine of Rome and Cyril of Alexandria of most holy memory, there should shine forth the exposition of the right and blameless faith by the 318 holy and blessed fathers gathered at Nice, at the time of Constantine of pious memory then emperor; and that what was defined by the 150 fathers at Constantinople to the removal of the heresies which had then sprung up, and the confirmation of the same our Catholic and Apostolic faith, should prevail."

Thereupon the two Creeds were recited.

Even after this, the Council of Chalcedon, in its Allocution to the Emperor Marcian [g], defending S. Leo against the charge of making additions to the faith, speaks of the Creed of the 318, as the *one* summary of teaching, which was given to the baptised.

[e] Conc. Eph. Act. vii.   [f] Conc. Chalc. Act. v. p. 1453. Col.
[g] Ib. P. iii. c. i. p. 1760. Col.

But the reception of the Creed, as a rule of faith, did not involve any liturgical or devotional use of it, which alone fixes it in the hearts of the people. The Council of Chalcedon, which received both Creeds, made no regulation as to any liturgical use of either, even in the East. On the contrary we are told that the Creed of the 318 fathers, which used to be recited on Maundy Thursday only by Candidates for Baptism, was first introduced into the office for Holy Communion, whenever used, by the heretical Patriarch of Antioch, Peter Gnapheus [h], (who died A.D. 486) and at Constantinople by a disreputable Patriarch, Timothy [i] (A.D. 511), as an implied censure on his expelled Predecessor. A very late writer [j], who, however, collected, he says, most of his materials from the Library of S. Sophia [k], and who mentions both accounts, must mean by "[l] the Creed of the 318" the Creed of Nice itself, (not the fuller Creed of Constantinople), since he speaks of one "[m] holding fast to *the other three Synods* which followed on the steps of the first."

Since there could be such unacquaintance with the Constantinopolitan Creed in Egypt, where the Greek language prevailed, much more in the West, for whom it must have been translated.

The West (in which the heresies of Novatian, Donatus, Jovinian, Pelagius were of a practical character, not relating to the Holy Trinity,) had for a long time no occasion for the Creeds either of Nice or Constantinople. "[n] The Churches of Africa,

[h] Theodorus Lector H. E. ii. 48.
[i] Id. ii. 32.   [j] Nicephorus Callistus A.D. 1333.
[k] Hist. Eccl. i. 1. p. 37.   [l] xvi. 35.   [m] Ib. c. 34.
[n] Lupus Conc. i. c. 4. in Pagi. A. 325. n. xxiv.

Italy, Gaul, retained the Apostles' Creed without any addition, as appears from Augustine, Chrysologus, Maximus of Turin, and other Latin Bishops, who delivered it alone to Catechumens. Theodoret, Sozomen, Socrates, attest that the Arian heresy could never pass the bound of Illyricum, and so the Europeans had no need of this new Profession; excepting only the Churches of Spain, invaded and seized by the Arian Goths Vandals and Suevi, [add the Visigoths and Burgundians] changed the Apostles' Creed into the Nicene, i.e. the Constantinopolitan, at the third Council of Toledo."

In like way, the "As it was in the beginning &c." was added to the " Glory be to the Father &c." on account of the Arian heresy, in the Council of Vaison A.D. 529, " as in other Churches."

In Italy we know that the Nicene Creed was not used in its public service before A.D. 1024. But neither is there any indication of its having been received elsewhere in the West.

Besides also that the West had no occasion for the Creed, its demur to the third Canon, "Let the Bishop of Constantinople have the precedence after the Bishop of Rome, because it is new Rome;" threw a slur upon the whole Council. Whether or no an Eastern Council was wise in altering the rank of the Eastern Patriarchs, without the consent of the West first obtained, the refusal of Rome to accept the Canon, and of the East to withdraw it, lessened the weight of the whole Council in the West in matters of faith too.

The Roman Synod of A.D. 484. in writing, as to matters of faith, "[o]to the orthodox presbyters and

[o] Conc. v. 248. Col.

archimandrites of Constantinople and Bithynia," speaks of its adherence "to the venerable synod of Nice and the 1st. of Ephesus and Chalcedon," but omits Constantinople. It is equally omitted in what seems to be the genuine form of the celebrated decree of Gelasius and the Roman Council A.D. 494 p.

The Canons of the Council of Nice remained the rule of the Spanish, as they were of the African Church. In the first Council of Toledo, A.D. 400, the presiding Bishop animadverts on the diversity of practice in the Spanish Churches, "reaching to schism," and suggests that "the enactments of the Council of Nice aforetime should be retained in perpetuity, and not be departed from q." The other 18 Bishops responded, that "if any one, knowing the acts of the Council of Nice, should presume to do otherwise, and persevere therein, he should be held as excommunicate, unless he amend his error, upon brotherly admonition."

Of the Council of Constantinople nothing is said.

The place which the Constantinopolitan Creed occupies in an old Gallican missal, supposed to be of the 7th century r, implies that it was not then used in the ordinary service. For it occurs, not in that service, but (in the Greek as well as Latin) in a service preparatory to Baptism, before Palm-Sunday.

The question addressed by the Presbyter in regard to those to be baptised, "In what language do

p See Ballerini de ant. Coll. can. Lat. c. xi. n. v. quoted by Hefele, Conc. Gesch. ii. 32.   q Conc. Tol. i. Conc. ii. 1471. Col.
r Thomasius Codd. Sacram. 900 annis vetustiores, Rom. 1680. Sacram. Rom. Eccl. i. n. xxxv. p. 54-56. On the date, see the preface of Thomasius.

they confess our Lord Jesus Christ? R. "In Greek," upon which the Acolythe chanted the Creed in Greek, implies that there was a Greek population, where this Creed was used; as the like question, subsequently asked and answered, "In Latin," implies that others were Latins. The Missal then probably represented one in the South of France, where Greeks and Latins were mixed, and so was of limited use.

S. Isidore of Seville, who, in the West, first mentions the Nicene Creed in his book " of Offices [a] " became Abp. of Seville A.D. 595, six years after the Council of Toledo.

But there can be no doubt of the entire loyalty and submission of all present from Spain (including Portugal) at the third Council of Toledo (A.D. 589) to the General Councils, specifically to that of Constantinople.

The Council consisted of two parts; the first was the public profession of the faith of the Arian Bishops and nobles recently converted. This was dictated to them by one of the Catholic Bishops, and was accepted and subscribed by the converts.

To preclude any suspicion of insincerity, they condemned, with anathema, Arianism as a whole, and several specific Arian or Macedonian denials of faith. But more largely, they condemned with anathema,

> "Whosoever believes that there is any other Catholic faith and communion, besides that of the universal Church, that Church which holds and honours the decrees of the Council of Nice, Constantinople, 1st of Ephesus, and Chalcedon."

[a] de off. i. 16. Opp. vi. 282.

Specifically, moreover, in four heads, they rejected with anathema, "any one who despised the faith of the Council of Nice;" "who does not say, that the faith of the 150 Bishops of the Council of Constantinople is true;" "who does not hold and take pleasure in the faith of the first Council of Ephesus and that of Chalcedon;" and more largely, "who does not receive all the Councils of orthodox Bishops consonant to those Councils;" again naming them.

Any who did not receive them sincerely would (as Pelagius did at the Synod of Diospolis) have condemned themselves.

They add,

> "This condemnation of the Arian faithlessness and communion, and of the Councils which cherish the Arian heresy, we have subscribed with our own hand, with anathema of them. The constitutions of the holy Councils of Nice, Constantinople, Ephesus, or Chalcedon, which we have heard with well-pleased ear and have approved as true by our confession, we have subscribed with our whole heart, our whole soul, our whole mind; thinking that nothing can be more lucid for the knowledge of the truth, than what the authorities of the aforesaid Councils contain. Of the Trinity and the Unity of Father, Son and Holy Ghost, nothing ever can be shewn to be clearer or more lucid than these."

Then they condemn,

> "Whoever should attempt to deprave, corrupt, change or depart from that Catholic faith and communion, which we have lately, in the mercy of God, obtained."

They then repeat "the Creed published at the Council of Nice;" "The holy faith, which the 150 fathers of the Council of Constantinople explained, consonant with the great Council of Nice;" and "The holy faith, which the tractators of the Council of Chalcedon explained."

The Creed, as they repeat and subscribe it, contains the clause, "We believe also in the Holy Ghost the Lord, and Giver of life, proceeding from the Father and the Son."

They were also fully aware of that provision of the Council of Ephesus, which some controversialists have been fond of declaring to forbid beforehand any such addition as the *Filioque*. For they embody the closing words of the Council of Chalcedon, which repeated it:

> "The holy and universal synod forbids to bring forward any other faith; or to write or believe or to teach other, or be otherwise minded. But whoso shall dare either to expound or produce or deliver any other Creed to those who wish to be converted to the knowledge of the truth from the heathen or Jews or any heretics whatsoever, if they be Bishops or Clerks, should be alien from the Episcopate or clergy; if monks or laymen, should be subject to anathema."

It is, of course, impossible to suppose that they can have believed *any* addition to the Creed to have been forbidden by this clause, and, accepting it with its anathema, themselves to have added to the Creed of Constantinople.

The intention of adhering to the Council of Constantinople is further expressed in the chapter, agreed upon by the whole Council, after the converted Bishops had been received; that provision, which has ultimately gained entrance for the Creed with this clause in the whole West.

"For reverence of the most holy faith, and for the strengthening of the weak minds of men, the holy Synod enacts, with advice of our most pious and most glorious Lord, king Recarede, that through all the Churches of Spain and Gallæcia the symbol of faith of the Council of Constantinople, i.e. of the 150 Bishops, should be recited according to the form of the Eastern Church; so that, before the Lord's prayer be said, it be sung with clear voice by the people: to the intent that the true faith should have a manifest testimony, and the hearts of the people approach, purified by faith, to taste the Body and Blood of Christ."

The only solution seems to be, that the Spanish Bishops knew of no other expression of doctrine, and that, accordingly, it had, in some way, found its way into their Latin translation of the Creed. For the liturgical use of the Creed, which, by the multiplication of copies and its universal use, made variation impossible, dated from this Council.

In the general Canon, confessing the Divinity of the Holy Ghost, proposed to the Council, the doctrine occurs as a part of the confession, as naturally as the denial of the Arian misbelief as to God the Son does in the preceding clause:

"Whosoever denies that the Son of God our Lord Jesus Christ was, without beginning, begotten of the substance of the Father and is equal to the Father or consubstantial, let him be anathema."

"Whosoever believeth not the Holy Ghost, or believeth not that He proceedeth from the Father and the Son, or saith not that He is coeternal with the Father and the Son, let him be anathema."

But the Spanish Church was already, in two ways familiar with what has become the Western confession of faith, "Who proceedeth from the Father and the Son."

i. "'A rule of the Catholic Faith against all heresies and especially against the Priscillianists, which the Bishops of Tarragona, Carthagena, Lusitania and Bætica made, and, with the precept of Leo, pope of the city of Rome, transmitted to Balconius, Bishop of Gallicia."

It was framed by the Bishops who enacted the canons of the first Council of Toledo[u]. It was framed on the type of the Nicene Creed, but with repeated rejection of the Sabellianism of the Priscillianists:

"We believe in One God, Father Son and Holy Ghost, Maker of all things visible and invisible, by Whom all things were created in heaven and in earth; that He is One God, and that this is One Trinity of Divine Substance: but that the Father is not the Son Himself, but hath a Son Who is not the Father; that the Son is not the Father; but that He is the Son of God, of [de] the Father's Nature; that the Spirit also is the Paraclete, Who is neither the Father nor the Son, but proceeding from the Father and the Son. The Father then is Unbegotten, the Son begotten; the Paraclete, not begotten, but proceeding from the Father and the Son &c."

Thus the doctrine of the Procession of the Holy Ghost from the Father and the Son was stamped as the belief of the whole of Spain, in a Creed which was framed against the domestic heresy, which was the great enemy of the truth in Spain, and so that

[t] Appended to the first Council of Toledo A.D. 400, but distinguished from it. Conc. II. 1475.

[u] This is stated in the sequel of the title.

doctrine was the more fixed in the minds of the Bishops and teachers of the Church.

ii. The other possible source of the clause is the Athanasian Creed. This was, from its form, framed to be chanted (as is implied by its other name "the Psalm *Quicunque*") and so this grand hymn became part of the devotion of the Latin Church. Its human author may remain unknown; but its language fixes it as belonging to the IVth or Vth century. It is inconceivable that so accurate a writer would not have used more definite language on the Nestorian and Eutychian heresies, had he lived after their rise [v]. He refutes them beforehand. In like way it has been observed, that S. Athanasius "[w] writes as precisely as if he had written after the Nestorian and Euthychian controversies, though without the technical words then adopted." But the author of the Creed does not use any of the special terms, which such a writer would have used, in allusion to them, after their appearance. It seems certain too, that after the spread of the Monophysite heresy, at the end of the Vth century, the writer would not have used the illustration, "For as the reasonable soul and flesh is one man," (which, although S. Augustine's [x], is not correct) since the Monophysites used it in support of their heresy [y]. The clause of the Creed, 'One, not by conversion of the Godhead into flesh, but by the taking of the Manhood into God,' although identi-

[v] See Waterland on the Ath. Creed c. 7. n. 1, 2.
[w] Dr. Newman on S. Ath. against Arians p. 244 n. 1. Oxf. Tr.
[x] Ep. 137. ad Volusian. c. 3. n. 11.
[y] The argument of Le Quien Diss. Dam. n. 17. p. 10. See also Waterland l. c. n. 4.

cal with a saying of S. Augustine[z], condemns the contrary heresy to that of Eutyches, who held that the Manhood was absorbed into God. It is inconceivable, again, that a statement of faith so carefully worded should have no allusion to Monothelism, had it been framed after the rise of that heresy.

Any one, who has looked over the statements on this doctrine, collected by Petavius and others from Latin writers of the Vth and VIth centuries must, I think, have been struck by the naked simplicity of their statements, as contrasted with the reasoning of S. Hilary, S. Ambrose and S. Augustine. At first sight, they disappointed me, as looking meagre. Observing however that two of the earlier, S. Paulinus and Prudentius, were connected with Spain, I cannot but think that the conciseness of the rest arises from their being repetitions of a common formula, that of the Athanasian Creed. They are a remarkable contrast with the rich and varied language of Greek fathers. Their identity with the Athanasian Creed lies on the surface. The language of S. Paulinus (A.D. 393) and Prudentius (A.D. 405) is varied by the necessities of the metre, in which they wrote. S. Paulinus has, "[a]And on His servants poured forth heavenly gifts, the Holy Spirit, proceeding from the Father and the Only-begotten;" Prudentius, "[b]Who our Lord, Who, Thine Only Son, breatheth the Paraclete from the Father's heart."

[z] "Verbum caro factum est, a Divinitate carne suscepta, non in carnem Divinitate mutata." Enchirid. c. 35.
[a] S. Paulin. in Nat. ix. S. Felic. ll. 91, 92.
[b] Cathemerinon. v. 159, 160.

The only two real variations which I have observed are, in a Creed attributed to S. Martin of Tours, (A.D. 375) probably also against the Priscillianists, and the anonymous writer known as Zachæus, probably Evagrius of about A.D. 400 [c].

S. Martin's Creed has;

> "[d] The Father in the Son, and the Son in the Father, and Both *in* the Holy Spirit."

Eucherius has;

> "[e] The Holy Ghost is in like way from the Father and the Son, in Person only and name not in majesty and substance to be accounted other; not Begotten as the Son, but proceeding from the Father, and of the same virtue Divinity honour and will, ever doing and bestowing all which the Father and the Son,—He, as He is ever *in* the Father and the Son, so the fulness of the Father and the Son ought to be believed to be in Him."

and, adapting the words of the 51st Psalm, "principalis Spiritus, rectus Spiritus, sanctus Spiritus," to the three Persons of the Holy Trinity, he says,

> "[f] [The Father] is the principal Spirit, because from Him is the only-Begotten Son, and from *Him* [ab Ipso, the Son] the Holy Spirit proceeding."

But after this time, the confession is one, the concise, "from the Father and the Son."

Thus Eucherius of Lyons A.D. 434;

> "[g] The Father is unbegotten, the Son begotten, the Holy Spirit neither begotten nor unbegotten. Lest if we should say, Unbegotten, we should seem to speak of two Fathers, or if Begotten, of

---

[c] Prof. Fidei facta a Martino Arch. Turon. in Bibl. Patr. v. 1084.
[d] See Gallandi Bibl. Patr. T. ix. Proleg. c. vi.
[e] Consult. Zachæi &c. L. ii. c. xix. Gall. ix. 239.
[f] Ib. ii. 3. p. 224.   [g] Quæst. Vet. Test. Qu. i. B. P. vi. 840.

two Sons; but rather Who proceedeth from the Father and the Son, as a sort of concord of the Father and the Son."

S. Leo (A.D. 440), full and accurate as he is, as a doctrinal writer, writing in detail against the Priscillianist errors and their Sabellianism, states the faith in the concisest form;

> "[h] They hold impiously as to the Divine Trinity, who assert that the Person of Father Son and Holy Ghost is one, as if the same God is called at one time the Father, at another the Son, at another the Holy Spirit, and there is not One Who begat, Another, Who is begotten, Another Who proceeded forth from Both, and the singular Unity is to be understood of three names, not of Three Persons."

Vigilius A.D. 480 as concisely;

> "[i] Hear more manifestly, that it is the property of the Father to have begotten: and the property of the Son to have been begotten; and the property of the Holy Ghost to proceed from the Father and the Son."

S. Fulgentius' testimony A.D. 493 is more remarkable from his repeating it with the same conciseness, so often;

> "[k] In this Holy Trinity, which is therefore repeated by us so often, that it may be fixed with greater sincerity in our heart, One is God the Father, Who alone essentially begat of Himself the One Son; and One Son, Who alone is essentially begotten of the One Father; and One Holy Spirit, Who Alone proceeds essentially of (de) the Father and the Son."

[h] Ep. xv. ad Turrib. c. i. ed. Ball.   [i] c. Eutych. Qu. 1.
[k] de fide ad Petr. c. i. Bibl. Pat. ix. 73.

And in the chapter on the Holy Spirit;

"¹ Believe most firmly and no wise doubt, that the same Holy Spirit, Who is the One Spirit of the Father and the Son, proceeds from (de) the Father and the Son."

And,

"ᵐ The Father is begotten of none; the Son is begotten of the Father; the Holy Spirit is proceeding from (a) the Father and the Son. The Father is not to Himself, but to the Son; the Son is not to Himself, but to the Father: the Spirit is of some one breathing; therefore their relative Names compose the Trinity.—Not diverse is the Essence of the Father and the Son and the Holy Spirit. If it were, neither would the Son be truly begotten of the Father; nor the Spirit proceed (a) from the Father and the Son. But because true is the Son, i. e. Begotten of the essence of the Father, true also is the Holy Spirit, proceeding from the Father and the Son. But if the Son or Holy Spirit are of another kind from the Father, neither is the Son truly the Father's, from Whom the different Essence would make Him alien. In like way neither would the Holy Spirit proceed from the Father and the Son, which it were mad to say; because Holy Scripture makes plain by a faithful relation, that both the Son is Begotten from the Father and the Spirit proceedeth from the Father."

And,

"ⁿ The Divinity of the Son could not receive the Holy Spirit, since the Holy Spirit Himself so proceedeth from the Son, as He proceedeth from the

---

¹ Ib. c. xi. p. 80, where he adduces proof from Holy Scripture.

ᵐ de Trin. c. 2. Ib. pp. 159, 160.

ⁿ de 5 quæstt. ad Ferrand. n. 26. Ib. p. 190. Petavius also says, "this is often repeated in the [39] fragments of the books against Fabian." Ib. n. 277-308.

Father, and is so given by the Son as He is given
by the Father; nor could that Nature, from which
the Holy Spirit hath Its origin, either wait for or
receive Its largess. That Spirit is whole of the
Father, and whole of the Son, because He is by
nature the One Spirit of the Father and the Son.
Wherefore He proceedeth whole [totus] from [de] the
Father and the Son; and He abideth whole in the
Father and the Son: for He so abideth that He
proceeds, and so proceeds that He abideth.—The
Divinity of the Son did not receive the Holy Spirit,
with which [Divinity] the Holy Spirit is of One
Nature, and from [ex] which He hath whatsoever
He hath, yea from [de] which He is what He is,
because what He by Nature hath, That He Is."

Gennadius, an Anti-Augustinian, (A.D. 495,)
opens his book "on the doctrines of the Church,"

"[o] We believe that there is One God, Father, Son
and Holy Ghost: Father, because He hath a Son;
Son, because He hath a Father; Holy Ghost, because He is from [ex] the Father and the Son. The
Father then is the Beginning [Principium] of Deity,
Who as He never was not God, so also was He
never not Father: from Whom the Son was Begotten; from [a] Whom the Holy Ghost was not Begotten, because He is not Son; nor Unbegotten, because He is not Father; nor made, because He is
not from [ex] nothing, but from [ex] God the Father and God the Son God proceeding."

Julianus Pomerius, A.D. 495,

"[p] Since we ought to instruct those same faithful,
who have been committed to us by God to be taught,
of the Father, how He alone is believed to be Unbegotten; of the Son, how He is Begotten of Him;

[o] De eccl. dogm. c. i. in S. Aug. Opp. T. viii. App. p. 75.
[p] de vita contempl. i. 18.

of the Holy Ghost, how, proceeding from [ex] the Father and the Son, He can neither be called Unbegotten nor Begotten; how these Three are One Substance; and this One Substance is not divided, but is distinguished into Three."

He proceeds in summary to speak of the Incarnation and of other articles of the Creed; so these are the heads of the teaching of Catechumens.

Paschasius, Deacon at Rome A. 501[q],

(The Holy Spirit) is said to be sent by the Father and the Son, and is known to proceed from [de] their substance and to do one work with them, and therefore the Son saith of Him, 'the Paraclete Who proceedeth from the Father.' He did not say, Who was created by the Father, but 'Who proceedeth from the Father,' that is, from being so associated with the power of the Father, and from His own proper nature. For the very saying, that He 'proceedeth from the Father' shews, that He, with the Father, has no beginning. But what means it, by its being said that the Son hath His birth from God the Father, and it is signified that the Holy Spirit proceeds? If you enquire, what difference there is between One Born and One Proceeding, evidently that He [the Son] hath His Birth from One, the Other goeth forth [progreditur] from [ex] Both.

Boethius A. 510[r],

"If you remember all which has been said above of God, let us think, that God the Son proceeded from [ex] God the Father, and the Holy Spirit from [ex] Both."

The statement of Pope Hormisdas, as contained in his Epistle to the Emperor Justin[s], A.D. 521. is

[q] de Sp. S. i. 12. Bibl. P. viii. 813.
[r] Ad Symm. de Trin. et unitate i. Opp. p. 11 fin. 27.
[s] Ep. 79. Justino Aug. Conc. v. 683.

the more remarkable, as having been addressed, after the ending of the schism, to that Emperor, as the summary of the faith of the General Councils, upon which he had desired to be instructed :

> "Great and incomprehensible is the mystery of the Holy Trinity, God the Father, God the Son, God the Holy Ghost, the undivided Trinity; and yet it is known that it belongeth to the Father, that He begetteth the Son; it belongeth to the Son of God, that He is begotten of the Father, equal to the Father; it belongeth to the Holy Spirit, that He proceedeth from [de] the Father and the Son, in the one Substance of the Godhead."

No exception is made to it by those in the East.

Ferrandus, a deacon of Carthage, A.D. 533 states it to be the Catholic faith against the Arians, who "subject the Son, as less, to the Father as greater; and believe the Holy Spirit to be inferior to the Son, being less:"

> "[t] The Catholics, on the contrary, not, like the Gentiles, to bring in three Gods, declare that God the Father, God the Son, God the Holy Ghost, have one honour, glory, greatness, eternity, divinity, equality, essence, and while they mean not to prefer one to the other, yet believe that the Son is born from the Father, that the Holy Spirit proceedeth [de] from the Father and the Son."

And to Severus, a Scholasticus of Constantinople, who enquired whether it might be said that One of the Holy Trinity suffered,

> "[u] To me, on account of the plain saying of the blessed Peter, who says generally to all the faithful, 'Be ready to give account to every one who asketh

[t] Ferrandi Epist. dogmat. adv. Arian. c. 2. in Maii Coll. nov. T. iii. P. ii. p. 171. Bibl. Patr. ix. 509.   [u] Id. Ib.

you of the faith which is in you,' it sufficeth to answer, that we believe in One God, Father Son and Holy Ghost; the Father, begotten by none; the Son, Only-Begotten from the Father; the Holy Spirit from [de] the Father Unbegotten, and the Son Only-Begotten, ever proceeding."

Agnellus, A.D. 462-556, Bishop of Ravenna A.D. 555, writing against the Arians,

"[v] Therefore the Son from [ex] the Father, the Holy Spirit proceedeth from [ex] the Father and the Son.—If there be this so great power in most frail man—how much more is it so in the omnipotence of God, that He should be the Almighty Father, the Begetter of the Son, and from [ex] Father and Son that Virtue proceeding, which is the Holy Spirit!"

S. Gregory Archbishop of Tours A.D. 573, opens his history with a confession of his faith, and says of God the Holy Ghost,

"I believe that the Holy Ghost proceeded from [a] the Father and the Son, not less, nor as though He before was not, but equal and ever with the Father and the Son co-eternal God, consubstantial in nature, equal in omnipotence, consempiternal in essence, so as never to have been without the Father and the Son, nor less than the Father and the Son."

It is in the next year after the Council of Toledo, viz. A.D. 590. that Pope S. Gregory I [w]. after the ancient custom of his predecessors, sent, on his ac-

[v] Ep. ad Armenium, Bibl. P. viii. 667.
[w] Vita S. Gregorii Pap. a Joh. Diac. scripta. Opp. iv. p. 45. Ben. John Diac. says, ii. 3 that "he *also* sent his Synodical to the 5 Patriarchs," in which he says, "I acknowledge and confess that I receive and venerate the four Councils, as I do the four books of the holy Gospel." c. 4.

cession, his confession of faith apparently to the other Patriarchs, varied somewhat from the Creeds, but based upon them:

> "I believe in One Almighty God, Father, Son and Holy Ghost, Three Persons, One Substance; the Father Unbegotten, the Son Begotten, the Holy Spirit, neither begotten nor unbegotten, but Co-eternal, Proceeding [de] from the Father and the Son."

All this naked identity of language implies, I think, an identity of a formula, whose language it is. And that formula, I doubt not, was the Athanasian Creed. If successive writers, in speaking of the Divinity of God the Son were to repeat, one after the other, "we believe that He is 'Very God of Very God'" and were to confine themselves to this one saying, no one, I think, would doubt that they were using the one formula of the Nicene Creed. As little room, I think, there is for doubting that these writers, using the one formula, "proceeding from the Father and the Son," were using the Athanasian. This S. Avitus (about A.D. 499) has, I think rightly, been understood [x] to say;

> "[y] We say that the Holy Spirit proceedeth from [a] the Son and the Father. The Lord Himself said, 'The Spirit of truth, Who proceedeth from [a] the Father.' For in that He saith, not 'proceeded'

---

[x] By Le Quien Diss. Dam. n. iv. p. iii. Waterland on the Ath. Creed, c. 7. p. 259. See also Rev. G. D. W. Ommanney, The Athanasian Creed p. 315. His work, (which is done with so much thoroughness) belongs, mostly, to a period, beyond that of this argument.

[y] Fragmenta libri de Divinitate Spiritus S. contra Gundobad. Arianum regem, published by Baluz. from an old MS in the Library of S. Gall. Gallandi Bibl. Patr. x. 793, 794.

but 'proceedeth,' He taught not any time of His proceeding, but, removing past and future, He shews the power of that Procession, in the eternity of an endless present; that, as it is the property of the Holy Spirit to proceed from [a] the Father and the Son, 'the Catholic Faith,' although it cannot persuade recusants of this, does not exceed in the rule of its discipline."

To most of us it would seem no effort of humility to think that the Benedictines were right in ascribing a certain sermon to Cæsarius Abp. of Arles [z], (A.D. 502.) It begins,

"I pray and admonish you, dearest brethren, that whoever wishes to be saved should learn the right and Catholic Faith, hold it firmly and keep it inviolate. So that every one ought to observe to believe the Father the Son and the Holy Ghost. The Father is God, the Son God, the Holy Ghost God, and yet not three Gods but One God. As is the Father, such is the Son, such also is the Holy Ghost. But let every faithful believe that the Son is equal to the Father as touching His Godhead, but inferior to the Father as touching the Manhood of the Flesh, which He took from us. But the Holy Spirit from Both proceeding."

Those who have been so anxious to divest the Athanasian Creed of its title of Creed, have overlooked that, in vindicating for it an old title, "the Psalm *Quicunque*," they have been vindicating also its use in public worship, from the time of its being. A Creed is not necessarily framed, in order to be recited. The Nicene Creed was not recited at first.

[z] Serm. 244. App. S. Aug. Opp. T. v. 399. Waterland (p. 259 note) says, that "Oudin [the Protestant] agrees with the Benedictines, Comm. de Scriptt. Eccl. i. 1348."

But a Psalm is composed with no other object than to be recited. And amid the difficulty of access to books the wide use of the language of the Athanasian Creed in early times, in itself, implies some common and public use of it. It seems to have pervaded the Breviaries. The Latin monks settled for piety at Mount Olivet A.D. 809, were Benedictines; for, in their letter to Leo III., they speak of the rule of S. Benedict, which they had received from Charlemagne. But they quote also the Athanasian Creed[a]. This affords a certain presumption that they recited it in their Psalter, in which it occurs on the Sunday at Prime. The Carthusians are said to observe the Benedictine rite [b]. They say the Athanasian Creed at Prime daily[c]. They are said in few things to differ from the Cistercians[c]. In the Roman Breviary of old, it was recited daily[d]. The Præmonstratensians hold theirs to be the old Roman Breviary[e]. The Ambrosian has much, which is peculiar to itself and is independent of others. In it the Athanasian Creed is recited at Prime daily[f]. S. Bernard, expressing surprise at an innovation of the Canons of Lyons, said, (about A.D. 1600,) that "[g] among the Churches of Gaul, that of Lyons hath been hitherto manifestly preeminent both in the dignity of its See, its worthy studies and laudable institutions. For where have careful discipline, gravity of manners, ripeness of counsels, weight of authority, marks of

[a] Published by Baluz. and, in full, Le Quien Diss. Dam. n. 13. pp. vi. vii.   [b] Bona de div. Psalm. xviii. 5. p. 622.
[c] Ib. p. 623.   [d] Honorius Gemma Animæ ii. 59.
[e] Bona l. c. n. 6. p. 624.   [f] Ib. 10. p. 631.
[g] Ep. 174 ad Canon. Lugd.

antiquity been equally found? *Especially in ecclesiastical offices* it has been seen never readily to acquiesce in sudden novelties; a Church, full of judgement, has not allowed itself to be tainted at any time by youthful levity." In this Church, so jealous of changes, Cardinal Bona says, that "[h] at Prime through the week, they only recite three Psalms, but on Lord's Days nine, *and the Athanasian Creed, which Creed all Churches have been wont to add to the Prime of the Lord's Day.*"

A Canon, "at the beginning of the 6th century imposed a penalty upon any Clergy, who neglect to learn the Athanasian Creed by heart;"

> "[i] First of all, let all Presbyters and Deacons or sub-deacons know by heart the Catholic Faith, and if any one neglects to do this, let them abstain for forty days from wine; but if, after the abstinence, they still neglect to commit it [to memory], let the sentence be repeated."

Penalties are not imposed, except on neglect. It must have been held to be a duty before; it would not have been at once sanctioned by a penalty. And the penalty in this case is to be continued, until the injunction is obeyed.

This would ensure that every priest of any weight would be familiar with the Athanasian Creed.

The West then, having at this time no other way of confessing the doctrine of the Holy Ghost than this, " Proceeding from the Father and the Son,"

[h] l. c. n. 9. p. 627.
[i] Epist. Canon. c. 1. in Docum. Juris Canon. Vet. in Baller. App. ad S. Leon. Opp. T. iii. p. 670. See Editorr. Obss. in Diss. xiv. Quesn. n. 2. coll. 955, 956. See also Ommanney n. 32 pp. 312, 313.

whether from the Athanasian Creed or from the former Council against the Priscillianists, it seems to me morally certain, that, whoever inserted it, supposed that the *Filioque* had dropped by mistake out of the Latin translation of the Nicene Creed, to which alone they probably had access in Spain at that time. Any one, in the least familiar with the collation of MSS, will be aware of this cause of change in the text of a father, that a scribe, bona fide, inserts, what he thinks has been accidentally omitted. Thus when the whole context relates to some contrast between the Father and the Son, a scribe will insert " et Spiritu Sancto " to complete the confession of the Trinity; the insertion has sometimes found its way into the printed text. In like way, I doubt not, the *Filioque* came into the translation, which was before the Bishops of the Third Council of Toledo, under a misapprehension, that it *must* be there. At the Council of Florence [k], the Latins produced " a very old MS " of the 2nd Council of Nice, which contained in the Creed the words, "and from the Son." If the words could have crept into a MS., which altogether misled Cardinal Julian, much more might the Bishops of the Council of Toledo, just breathing again from the Arian oppression, be bona fide mistaken. But a " mistake " is neither an "irregularity," nor, if unavoidable, " a fault." The Bishops of the 3rd Council of Toledo acted, in intention, dutifully to the Council of Constantinople; the mistake was not discovered until 200 years after.

The Devotional use of the Nicene Creed in the

[k] Conc. Flor. Sess. v.

West began with this Council of Toledo. From the connection of ritual between France and Spain, the custom of singing the Creed at the Holy Communion spread into France; and wherever it spread, it spread in this enlarged form, in which alone they knew it. No doubt was raised as to the clause, because it was the one expression of the faith in the West. The Latin monks at Mount Olivet, when disturbed by some Greek monks of the monastery of S. Saba, appealed to its use in the chapel of Charlemagne. They said in their Epistle to Leo III., "[1] Would you vouchsafe to inform the Emperor Charles your son, that we heard those words in his chapel, 'Who proceedeth from the Father and the Son?'" Charlemagne had, at this time, a somewhat indefinite title, (accorded to him by the Saracens) "Protector of the Holy Land." The Council of Aix sent, as you know, two deputies to Leo III. Leo III. says that he would not have inserted the words; "[m] for I would not, I say not, set myself above" the framers of the Creed, "illumined both with human and Divine knowledge, but far be it from me even to equal myself to them!" He advised even to remove the words. Yet when the deputies urged, "if language full of right faith be removed, will not that same language be condemned by all, as though contrary to the faith?" he said, "had I been asked, before it was so sung, I would have answered that it should not be inserted;" but, as it was, he suggested, that "the singing of the Creed in the palace

[1] Epist. peregr. Monach. in Monte Oliveti ad Leon. Pap. published by Le Quien Diss. Damasc. p. vi.
[m] Conc. Aquisgr. A. 809. Conc. ix. p. 278 sqq. Col.

should gradually be intermitted, since it is not sung in our holy Church, in the hope that it might gradually be disused by all." The love, however, of the Creed, or the dread of injuring the faith prevailed, and the singing of the Creed continued. No one, I should think, could blame the French Bishops for this fear. Leo III. too saw, that the words, "and the Son," could not be left out, without risk to the faith; and finally advised, not the omission of the words, but the disuse of the custom of singing the Creed. And so the Creed continued to be sung in Spain, France and Germany, for the next 400 years, during which it was not received at Rome; when at last, on the importunity of the Emperor Henry, it was received unwillingly. "The Romans," says an eye-witness of its first introduction[n], "did not sing the Creed after the Gospel to these times of the Emperor Henry of blessed memory." "The Emperor ceased not pressing it, until, with the consent of all, he persuaded the Lord Benedict of the Apostolic see, that they should sing it at the public mass." "From the year 1014," says Card. Bona[o], "the Creed began to be sung at Rome, by the direction of Benedict VIII, and so neither in the Ordo Romanus, nor in ancient Mss. Sacramentaries, nor in Alcuin [A.D. 784], Amalarius [A.D. 816], Rabanus [A. D. 847], Remigius Antissiod. [A. D. 880], or others who, before the aforesaid year, explained the service of the Roman Mass, is there any mention of the Creed; whereas it was sung, long before, in Spain France and Germany. It is found also

---

[n] Berno Augiensis lib. de reb. aliquot ad missam pertin. c. 2. Bibl. Patr. xviii. 57.   [o] Rerr. Liturg. L. ii. c. 8. n. 2.

in all the Liturgies of the Greeks, Maronites and other nations in the East."

Whether the Bishop of Rome ever formally received the altered Creed, there are no documents to shew. Photius seems to have inferred that he did, because the Latin Bishops, in teaching the Bulgarians the doctrine of the Holy Trinity, taught the Procession from the Father and the Son. But Latins, if they taught the doctrine of Holy Ghost at all, had no other way, in which to teach it. Photius declaims against this as a heresy. For he sums up, "ᵖ This ungodliness those Bishops of darkness (for they alleged that they were Bishops,) disseminated among the Bulgarians, together with those other unlawful things. The report of these came to our ears." It was then report only. His charge is; "ᑫ Besides the aforesaid absurdities, they undertook to adulterate with spurious thoughts and interpolated words the sacred and holy Creed, which, by the decree of all the Œcumenical synods, has an impregnable force, (O the machinations of the Evil one!) using new phrases, that the Holy Spirit proceedeth not from the Father only, but from the Son also." But he continues to declaim, not as to the technical charge of adding to the Creed, but as to the doctrine itself (which he misinterprets), as "ungodly and diabolic."

But, any how, Photius himself stated exactly the contrary, that Pope Nicolas did *not* add to the Creed. He says, "ʳ He did not dare, with bare head, to

---

ᵖ Phot. Encycl. Ep. [Ep. 2] p. 54.   ᑫ Ib. n. 8-23.

ʳ Phot. tract. de Proc. Sp. S. cont. Latinos, fin.

array himself against those most excellent things; but neither did he, making the aweful Creed a veil for his meaning, to be carried about on the lips of all, clip or maltreat the aforesaid most pious and honoured work of the Churches."

Again, in the Epistle which he forged in the name of John VIII., he makes John say, "*You know, brother, how when he, whom you sent lately, came to us, and consulted us about the sacred Creed, he found that we preserve it unshaken, as it was delivered to us from the beginning, and neither added to it nor subtracted from it." In this he is speaking of the Creed, not of the faith of the Latins; for he continues to make John speak of "the subverters of the Theology of Christ the Lord, and of the holy Pontiffs and the other holy Fathers, who meeting in Synod delivered the sacred Creed to us." Photius makes John VIII. say, that he "preserved" it; he therefore, here too, tacitly retracts his statement, that Nicolas I. changed it.

In a yet later letter [A. 883] to a Bishop of Aquileia, he refers to the Synod at Constantinople, at which John's legates were present and signed the Greek Creed (as there was no reason why they should not), though he interprets it as a renunciation of the belief in the double Procession, which he attributes to "ᵘ a few only in the West."

Baronius endeavours in vain to find any Pope,

---

* The Epistle is given in Baronius A. 879. liv-lviii. T. 15 pp. 356, 7 and in the Councils. Weak and straitened by political circumstances as John VIII. was, it is incredible that he wrote such a letter, the falsifications and forgeries of Photius being notorious.

ᵗ Ep. ad Episc. Aquil. n. 25. in Combefis Bibl. Patr. Auct. Nov. i. 536.   ᵘ Ib. n. 3. p. 528.

to whom the "formal addition" may be ascribed [v], and rests at last on a statement of a writer towards the end of the 12th century, writing against the Greeks. "[w] If the Council of Constantinople added to the Nicene Creed, 'in the Holy Ghost, the Lord, and Giver of life,' and the Council of Chalcedon to that of Constantinople, 'perfect in Divinity and perfect in Humanity, consubstantial with the Father as touching His Godhead, consubstantial with us as touching His Manhood,' and some other things as aforesaid, the Bishop of the elder Rome ought not to be calumniated, because for explanation, he added one word (that the Holy Spirit proceeds from the Son,) having the consent of very many Bishops and most learned Cardinals." "For the truth of which," says Le Quien[x], "be the author responsible!" It seems to me inconceivable, that all account of any such proceeding, if it ever took place, should have been lost [y].

Cerularius, who renewed the schism, alleged nothing at first of any addition to the Creed by the Latins. On the contrary Peter of Antioch defends him, that he did not

> "call the Westerns heterodox or cut them off from the holy Catholic Church, but knowing well that

---

[v] A.D. 883. n. xxxiv-xxxviii.   [w] Hugo Etherianus (A.D. 1177) de hæres. quas Græci in Latinos devolvunt iii. 16. Bibl. Max. Patr. xxii. 1252.   [x] Disc. Dam. n. 28. p. xv.

[y] At the Council of Florence the Latin Bishop of Rhodes even said that "this unfolding of the Creed took place in a number of so many Western Bishops in the presence of the Pope, who hath the power of convening Bishops, as is shewn by your [the Greek] witnesses too," so that "it did not seem necessary that the others should come," but contends that it did not appear that they were

they were orthodox and of one mind with us as to the safe theology, touching the life-originating and Consubstantial Holy Trinity, and the Incarnation of our Lord and God and Saviour Jesus Christ, they stumbled in this one thing, that they used unleavened bread at the oblation[1]."

However, afterwards, he revived the charge of Photius about the addition to the Creed, it was but an after-thought, in the progress of the schism.

It is, plainly a distinct question, whether it would not have been lawful for the Western Church to have added to the Creed for their own use, as the Greek Church, for *their* use, added at Constantinople to the Creed of Nicæa. The Greek Church, until the Council of Chalcedon, was in the same condition relatively to the West, as the Westerns are now to the East. The Council of Constantinople became a General Council, because its Creed was, after 71 years, accepted by the whole Church. The Council was not acknowledged by the Council of Ephesus, as neither did the Council of Ephesus receive its Creed. It was received on the ground of its sound exposition of the faith, which the Council of Chalcedon accepted for the whole Church: that faith was not accepted upon *its* authority.

The subsequent reception of the Creed of Constantinople by the Latins does not alter the original fact, that that Creed was first framed, upon the

---

not invited, nor was the Roman Church obliged to invite them. (Sess. viii. Conc. xviii. p. 125, Col.). Yet of this Council there is not a trace.

[1] Peter Antioch. Ep. ad Domin. Grad. n. 7. Coteler. Eccl. Gr. monum. T. ii. p. 117.

model of the Nicene Creed, by the Greeks for themselves, to meet heresies, which had sprung up among them. The case was urgent. Perhaps, in the then state of disharmony between the Churches of Antioch and Rome, it was impossible to wait for the Latins, or for the Greek Emperor to invite the Latins. Had this been done, who knows but that the Creed of Constantinople might have been so worded, that this question as to the *Filioque* might never have arisen? But any how the principle was established, that the East might, for its own necessities, modify the existing Creed [the Nicene]. Even then if those in the West, instead of receiving the *Filioque* under a mistaken idea of dutifulness, had introduced the *Filioque*, on any ground of necessity, for their own use, I do not see how this would have been different from the act of the 150 fathers of Constantinople A.D. 451. They were not a General Council *then*, but a Greek Council.

So long then as the Latins did not attempt to force the addition upon the Greeks, I cannot see, why they might not have used, without blame, the same formula in the Nicene Creed, which they already had in the Athanasian. It would have been strange that our Western priests should have had to confess in their early prayers, that "the Holy Ghost proceeded from the Father and the Son," and then in the Communion-service to have confessed, "Who proceedeth from the Father." This difference could not, I think, have continued. The Latins need not have sung the Nicene Creed at all. It was an act of devotion adopted from the Greek Church, and intended to assimilate us to it. When the discrepancy was discovered, there was no remedy, without injury to the faith of the people. Leo III, on this ground, advised, not the omission of the clause, while the use of the Creed remained, but the omission of the Creed altogether. Devotion, however, prevailed. The Nicene Creed held its ground, against the advice of the Pope; and while it remained, all thought it to be a necessity, that the clause should remain also.

Since, however, the clause, which found its way into the Creed, was, in the first instance, admitted, as being supposed to be part of the Constantinopolitan Creed, and, since after it had been rooted for 200 years, it was not uprooted, for fear of uprooting also or perplexing the faith of the people, there was no *fault* either in its first reception or in its subsequent retention.

The Greeks would condemn forefathers of their own, if they were to pronounce the clause to be heretical. For it would be against the principles of the Church to be in communion with an heretical body. But from the deposition of Photius A.D. 886 to, at least, A.D. 1009, East and West retained their own expression of faith without schism [a].

A.D. 1077, Theophylact did not object to the West, retaining for itself the confession of faith contained in the words, but only excepted against the insertion of the words in the Creed:

"[b] In all besides, I will allow you to use this word,

[a] Peter of Antioch, about A. 1054, says that he had heard the name of the Roman Pontiff recited from the diptychs at the Mass at Constantinople, 45 years before. Le Quien. p. xii.

[b] in Joann. Vccc. Orat. i. de union. Eccl. in Leo Allat. Græcia Orthod. pp. 218, 219.

'the proceeding of the Spirit from the Father and the Son,' as speech enableth thee; I mean, in common discourses and ecclesiastical homilies, if thou willest; in the Symbol alone I will not grant thee."

In 1155 Basil Achridenus Archbishop of Thessalonica "[c]a man of great name at that time in the Eastern Church," wrote to Adrian II, "we teach and preach the same, I and all who belong to the great and Apostolic See of Constantinople; and one and the same word of faith soundeth in both Churches, [d] although some slight stumbling-blocks separated us." And this he wrote, having apparently in his mind our Western accession to the Creed; for he speaks of the Greeks, as "innovating in nothing from the Synodical decrees, nor adding jot or tittle to the words of the Gospels and Epistles;" which is the usual way of the Greeks in speaking of it.

The Bishops in the time of the Emperor John Ducas (A.D. 1249) proposed that "[e]the interpolation should be put out of the Creed, but might be retained and used in any other form." (A.D. 1256) Alexander IV rehearsed the terms of union proposed to his predecessor Innocent IV, who disapproved indeed that this article of the Nicene Creed ("[f]'in which the Greek Church seems to disagree a very little from the Roman") was excepted from the Council to be held, but granted that

> "in the approaching Council the tenor of the aforesaid Creed should not be changed except by mutual consent, which, we hope, the harmony of

[c] Baron. A. 1155. xxx.   [d] βραχέα τινα προσκόμματα, Greek in Jur. Gr. Rom. v. 307, Lat. in Baron. l. c.
      [e] Pachymeres v. 12. T. i. p. 375. Bonn.
   [f] Le Q. p. xxi. from Wading i. 147, Regest. Lib. ii. Ep. 325.

reconciliation will bring, but should, in the Greek Church, remain in that form, in which the Synod aforesaid promulgated it, provided that, as to the faith in the Holy Trinity, the Greek Church have throughout the same Catholic Faith [in omnibus catholicè consentiat] as the Roman."

The "understanding" finally arrived at, at the 2nd Council of Lyons (A.D. 1274), was that each should retain their own form [g].

Even at the beginning of the Council of Florence, Mark of Ephesus, who in the end made it fruitless, said,

"[h] Efface it from the confession of faith and let it be placed where you will, and let it be sung in the Churches as the hymn, 'The Only-Begotten Word of God, being immortal.'"

The Latins answered well;

"If the addition have blasphemy, shew it, and we will efface it both from the Holy Creed, and from all the books, in which the holy fathers wrote of theology, Cyril, Ambrose, Gregory [Naz.], Gregory [Nyss.], Basil, Jerome, Augustine, Chrysostom, and very many more. But if we Latins confessing one Beginning and cause and fountain and root, the Father, of the Son and Holy Spirit, not making two Beginnings, what need of effacing the addition? For we do not call it an addition, but an explaining and unfolding."

Unless it were heresy, it would be a mere childish piece of etiquette, to demand its removal. Photius invented a new heresy, which he assumed to lie in it, and consistently required its removal. Nechites, after his conference with Anselm of Havelberg about A.D. 1149, when satisfied as to the

[g] See ab. p. 14.   [h] Duc. Hist. c. 32. p. 214. Bonn. Conc. Flor. Sess. xv.

identity of the Greek and Latin Confessions, only desired the authority of a General Council, to be held hereafter, to prevent scandal from the reception of the word, hitherto unused in Greek Creeds [i]. He had no objection to the Latins using their form for themselves.

I should hope then that the Eastern Church would be satisfied with some such statement as this, in lieu of the Bonn Preliminary Proposition 3.

"We agree together in acknowledging that the addition of the *Filioque* in the Latin copies of the Niceno-Constantinopolitan Creed, having come in under a wrong impression that it was part of the Creed, settled by the Council of Constantinople, and not having itself the authority of any General Council, ought never to have been enforced upon the Greek Church."

None on our side could object to such a simple statement.

I have, I trust, removed the imputation that there was any wilful interpolation of the Creed; or that the present form of our Western Creed is owing to any arbitrary act of the Bishop of Rome, which is so often repeated, and which even our own learned and good Bishop Pearson (to whom in early days we have all owed so much) too readily believed, on the self-contradicted statement of Photius, whose own character was in those days inadequately known.

There is one other allegation, which has often been interposed to hinder or bias the consideration of the doctrine of the *Filioque*, viz. that the Council of Ephesus forbade, it is said, any future expansion

[i] See ab. p. 16.

of the Creed. It did nothing less; as indeed it would have been extreme presumption in any number of men, however gifted, unless gifted with omniscience, to do this. It would go beyond a mere claim of infallibility as to any given doctrine. For it would require a Divine prescience, that no error would arise in the Church, against which it might be necessary to guard by any fresh definition. Almighty God, Who alone knows the future of His Church, could alone know this.

The occasion of the oft-cited decree of Ephesus was this. Two Nestorian presbyters of Constantinople, Anastasius and Photius, had given commendatory letters, attesting the orthodoxy of two other Nestorians, Antonius and James, addressed to the Bishops of Lydia. There were at that time many Quartodecimans and Novatians, who wished to return to the Church. This James, "deceiving," as Charisius alleged, " some of the simpler " sort, setting at nought the exposition of faith of the holy fathers at Nice, made them subscribe a Creed, of ostentatious orthodoxy on the doctrine of the Trinity, but using exclusively the Nestorian formula, "[k] conjunction with the Divine Nature," whereby the Nestorians evaded the doctrine of the Incarnation. Some, not named, had excommunicated Charisius, who, as Œconomus of Philadelphia, had excepted against this. They had also attested the orthodoxy of James. Charisius appealed to the Council. The exposition of the transformed Creed (as it is

[k] συνάφεια. This word is repeated five times in the Nestorian Creed. See on the Nestorian use of the word, Petav. de Incarn. iii. 3. Marius Mercator, a contemporary, who translated the

called in the Acts) was read, with the signatures of those who had been induced to sign it, as "the true faith of orthodoxy," praying the most holy Bishop Theophanes to receive them into the most holy Catholic Church.

"These things being read, the holy synod defined that it was unlawful to propose or compose or put together another (ἑτέραν) faith, beside (παρὰ) that defined by the holy fathers, gathered at Nice with the Holy Spirit; and that those who dared either to compose or propose or offer to those who wish to return to the knowledge of the truth, either from heathenism or Judaism or any heresy whatsoever, another faith, if Bishops or Clergy, should be alien from the episcopate or Clergy, or, if laymen, should be anathematised."

"In like way, if any Bishops or Clergy should be detected, holding or teaching the doctrines contained in the exposition, brought before [the Council] by the Presbyter Charisius concerning the Incarnation of the Only-Begotten Son of God, viz. the wicked and perverted doctrines of Nestorius, which also are subjoined, let them be subject to the sentence of this holy Œcumenical Synod (repeating it)."

It is obvious, from the history itself, that the prohibition is to individual arbitary acts. It is, that "*no one* shall be allowed," and the Council annexes an individual penalty to the transgressors of their decree, degradation or excommunication. It is almost superfluous to say, that it was the substitution of a heretical Creed, which was proscribed.

Creed into Latin, calls it (as knowing it to be so) the Creed of Theodorus of Mopsuestia: Charisius apparently did not know, any how did not name, its author.

There is not an indication that the Council thought that they could fetter the free action of the Church, or meant to do so. Even with these limitations, all which is forbidden is, to substitute for the Nicene any such different Creed in receiving Jews heathen or heretics into the Church. It obviously could not mean to prohibit *true* additions to the Creed of Nice. For the only Creed, which the Council of Ephesus received, was the actual Creed of Nice, which they rehearsed at the beginning of this session. On that other construction they would have condemned the fathers of the Council of Constantinople, whose Creed they did not themselves receive. For these *did* add to the Nicene Creed, and require subscription to the Creed so augmented.

It became the habit of Eastern heretics to allege this decree, which was framed on occasion of a heretical Creed, to protect their own heresies from condemnation. But the heretics did not except against Creeds only. They pleaded the Canon against any positive statement of doctrine, which was not contained, in terms, in the Nicene Creed. Eutyches, we saw, pleaded it against any enquiry as to his faith, made to him by Flavian[1]. Some of the Bishops at the Council of Chalcedon had also taken part in the Robber-Council, and dreaded what might follow. They had themselves taken part with Dioscorus, in using the Canon for the unjust condemnation of S. Flavian. There was frequently the cry in the Council, especially from the Illyrian Bishops, "[m]We have all erred: may we all find forgive-

---

[1] See ab. p. 38, 39.
[m] Act. i. fin. Conc. iv. 1191. Act. ii. Ib. 1240. bis.

ness." When then the judges and senate proposed,

> "[n] If your reverences please, let the most holy patriarchs of each diocese choose in addition one or two, each of his own diocese, and having consulted in common about the faith, establish openly what seems good to all:

it was probably these same who cried out,

> "We make no written exposition. A canon says plainly, that what has been set forth, sufficeth. The canon wills, that there should not be another exposition. Let the things of the fathers hold."

Any how, after the Epistle of S. Leo had been read, and three passages made clear by aid of passages of S. Cyril, there was no further question; but a "written exposition," the tome of S. Leo, being found in harmony with S. Cyril and the Council of Ephesus, was accepted by that of Chalcedon.

The Monophysites continued to plead the Canon against the Council of Chalcedon, which, against error, added to credenda, not to the Creed.

Eulogius, Archbishop of Alexandria, (A.D. 581) shewed very clearly that the objection would lie to every Council which laid down any thing as to the faith, even the Council of Ephesus itself, as also to that of Constantinople:

> "[o] Again, the madness of heresy blames the 4th Council for setting forth an exposition, maintaining that any such attempt is wholly precluded by the first Council of Ephesus. And yet if, according to their idle speech, that Council had altogether forbidden making another definition, it would, before all others, have passed a sentence of condemnation

---

[n] Act. ii. init. p. 1208.
[o] Eulog. in Phot. Bibl. cod. 230. p. 275, 1. Bekk.

against itself. For it *does* define what none before it defined. Nay its ἡ καθ' ὑπόστασιν ἕνωσις is a definition, not made by the elder Synods. Yea, and in the vain speech a false charge is brought against the Synod of the 150 holy fathers at Constantinople; for it, putting down the rebel against the Spirit, and adding the theology as to the Holy Spirit to the definition expressed at Nice, conjoined it therewith. For if the previous Councils, with their additions, escape blame, neither will those, after them, for the like acts have an unlike condemnation. So does this senselessness confuse and distort everything. For the Council of Ephesus wholly forbade that another faith should be set forth, whose dogmas were contrary[p] to that at Nice; but what was defined by it being maintained pure and inviolate, to add what was required by circumstances was what it did itself. And this is the teaching of nature itself, and the tradition of the Church throughout is seen to acquiesce in this. Wherefore also at Alexandria, before the Ecumenical Synod was convened, the divine Cyril, having gathered there select Bishops and having framed a written statement of faith, sent it to Nestorius."

S. Maximus, the Confessor, A.D. 456, had to answer the same imputation from the Monophysites, as to "the confession of two natures of our Lord," and the term "in two natures," in the Council of Chalcedon. He answers,

"[q] How and with what reason do you accuse the holy Council of Chalcedon, although it manifoldly useth the words of the fathers, and abuse it and mock it as though it introduced another definition of the Faith?—If the Council of Chalcedon may be accused of making another definition of the Faith,

[p] ἧς ἐναντία τὰ δόγματα.   [q] Opp. ii. 141, 142.

on account of the words inserted in the Nicene definition, the same may be said against Cyril also, and the 150 fathers [the third and the second General Council]. How it should *not* lie against them, and *should* lie against this [of Chalcedon], I comprehend not.—For Gregory, the defender of the Faith, will not any more escape your accusation against those of Chalcedon; rather he will lie under it exceedingly, expressing distinctly what was deficiently said as to the Holy Spirit by the Council of Nice, 'because,' he says, 'this question had not yet been mooted.'—If we may speak the truth, all the God-elected fathers after the Council of Nice, and every Council of orthodox and holy men, did not, through the introduction of words of their own, introduce another definition of the Faith, as you declare;—but they firmly established that one and the same faith which was laid down by the 318 fathers, elucidating and, as it were, explaining it in detail, on account of those who understood it amiss and misinterpreted[r] it and its doctrines to their own ungodliness."

S. Cyril ought to understand the canon, which he probably himself framed, as presiding over the Council of Ephesus, as Archbishop of Alexandria and representative of Celestine, Bishop of Rome. His signature immediately succeeds the Canon[s]. We can hardly think that we understand it better than he who probably framed it, nay who presided over the Council which passed it. He however, explained that what was not *against* the Creed was

[r] S. Maximus contrasts the "additional interpretations" of the Church (ἐπεξηγούμενοι) and the "misinterpretations" (παρεξηγούμενοι) of heretics, which may illustrate what was forbidden by the παρὰ of the Council of Ephesus.

[s] Conc. Eph. Act. vi. T. iii. p. 1221. Col.

not *beside* it. The Orientals had proposed to him as terms of communion, that he should "do away with all he had written in epistles tomes or books, and agree with that only faith which had been defined by our holy Fathers at Nice." "But," S. Cyril wrote back,

> "[t] we all follow that exposition of faith which was defined by the holy fathers in the city of Nice, sapping absolutely nothing of the things contained in it. For they are all right and unexceptionable; and anything curious, after it, is not safe. But what I have rightly written against the blasphemies of Nestorius no words will persuade me to say that they were not done well:"

and against the imputation that he "had received an exposition of faith or now Creed, as dishonouring that old and venerable Creed," he says [u],

> "Neither have we demanded of any an exposition of faith, nor have we received one newly framed by others. For Divine Scripture suffices us, and the prudence of the holy fathers, and the symbol of faith, framed perfectly as to all right doctrine. But since the most holy Eastern Bishops differed from us as to that of Ephesus and were somehow suspected of being entangled in the meshes of Nestorius, therefore they very wisely made a defence, to free themselves from blame, and eager to satisfy the lovers of the blameless faith, that they were minded to have no share in his impiety; and the thing is far from all note of blame. If Nestorius himself, when we all held out to him that he ought to condemn his own dogmas and choose the truth instead thereof, had made a written confession there-

[t] Ep. 35 ad Acac. Melit. Opp. v. P. ii. 2. p. 110.
[u] Ib. p. 112, 113.

on, who would say that he framed for us a new exposition of faith? Why then do they calumniate the assent of the most holy Bishops of Phœnicia, calling it a new setting forth of the Creed, whereas they made it for a good and necessary end, to defend themselves and soothe those who thought that they followed the innovations of Nestorius? For the *holy Œcumenical Synod gathered at Ephesus provided, of necessity, that no other exposition of faith beside that which existed, which the most blessed fathers, speaking in the Holy Ghost, defined, should be brought into the Churches of God.* But they who at one time, I know not how, differed from it, and were suspected of not being right-minded, following the Apostolic and Evangelic doctrines, how should they free themselves from this ill-report? by silence? or rather by self-defence, and by manifesting the power of the faith which was in them? The divine disciple wrote, 'be ready always to give an answer to every one who asketh you an account of the hope which is in you.' But he who willeth to do this, innovates in nothing, *nor doth he frame any new exposition of faith*, but rather maketh plain to those who ask him, what faith he hath concerning Christ."

The fathers of the Council of Chalcedon, by their practice, are authoritative exponents of the Canon of Ephesus. For they renewed the prohibition of the Council of Ephesus to "adduce any other faith;" but, in "the faith" which is not to be set aside, they included not only the Creeds of Nice and Constantinople, but the definitions at Ephesus and Chalcedon itself. The statements of the faith were expanded, because fresh contradictions of the faith had emerged. After directing that both Creeds should be read, the Council says,

"This wise and saving Symbol of Divine grace

would have sufficed to the full knowledge and confirmation of the faith; for it teaches thoroughly the perfect truth of the Father Son and Holy Ghost, and presents to those who receive it faithfully the Incarnation of the Lord. But since they who take in hand to annul the preaching of the truth have through their own heresies generated empty sayings [they describe Nestorianism and Eutychianism]; therefore this present great holy and Ecumenical Council, wishing to shut out every device against the truth, teaching thoroughly the unshaken truth, proclaimed from the beginning, has defined preeminently that the faith of the 318 fathers should remain unassailed, and, on account of those who fought against the Holy Ghost, confirms the teaching concerning the Substance of the Holy Ghost, delivered subsequently by the 150 holy fathers who met in the royal city, which they make known to all, not as introducing any thing wanting to those before them, but making clear by testimonies of Scripture this conception of the Holy Spirit against those who wished to annul His being Lord: and moreover on account of those who took in hand to corrupt the mystery of the Dispensation, and who shamelessly fabled that He, Who was born of the holy Mary, was mere man, it received the Synodical Epistles of the blessed Cyril, who was shepherd of the Church of Alexandria, to Nestorius and the Easterns, being adapted to refute the phrenzy of Nestorius, and as an interpretation for those who with pious zeal desire to understand the saving Creed; to which also they reasonably conjoined the epistle of the president of the greater Rome, the most blessed and holy Archbishop Leo, which he wrote to the Archbishop Flavian now among the saints, for the destruction of the evil-mindedness of Eutyches, as agreeing with the confession of the great Peter, and as a column against both misbelievers in common, to the confirmation of the orthodox doctrine."

Then, having in detail shewn how both heresies were confuted by it, and having set forth the true doctrine, they sum up,

> "These things being framed by us with all accuracy and care on every side, the holy and œcumenical Synod defines, that it shall be lawful for no one to produce or compose, or put together, or hold, or teach others another faith, and those who venture &c." (as in the Council of Ephesus)

The Council of Chalcedon enlarged greatly the terms although not the substance of the faith contained in the Nicene Creed: and *that*, in view of the heresies which had since arisen; and yet renewed in terms the prohibition of the Canon of Ephesus and the penalties annexed to its infringement. It shewed, then, in practice, that it did not hold the enlargement of the things proposed as *de fide* to be prohibited, but only the producing of things contradictory to the faith once delivered to the saints.

Its prohibition, moreover, to "hold" another faith shews the more, that they meant, only to prohibit any contradictory statement of faith. For if they had prohibited any additional statement, not being a contradiction of its truth, then (as Cardinal Julian acutely argued in the Council of Florence[v]) any one would fall under its anathema, who held (as all must) any thing not expressed in set terms in the Nicene Creed; such as that God is eternal or incomprehensible.

The alleged plea for the condemnation of S. Fla-

[v] Conc. Flor. Act. xi. Conc. xviii. 175. Col.

vian and Eusebius of Dorylæum in the Robber-Council was the infringement of this Canon of the first Council of Ephesus. Dioscorus put the question,

> "[w] I think that you all approve what was set forth by the holy fathers who met at Nice of old, which also the holy Synod formerly collected here confirmed, and decreed should alone hold and were sufficient. We heard them defining thus, 'If any one speaks or thinks, or prepares, or seeks beside these things, let him be subject to condemnation.' What think you? Let each say in writing, of what mind he is. Can we seek or prepare beside these things? If any have sought beyond what was said, will he not be justly subjected to the sentence of the fathers? Let each say, if he is of this mind."

In answer, some of the Bishops only expressed their adherence to the faith of Nice and Ephesus; others pronounced, according to the mind of Dioscorus, that those who exceeded that faith were aliens from or enemies to the Catholic faith. Dioscorus then repeating the Canon of Ephesus and its sentence, and setting forth generally the confusions caused by S. Flavian and Eusebius, that they had become the occasion of scandal and disturbance to the holy Churches and orthodox people every where, said, "it is plain that they have subjected themselves to the penalties then synodically decreed by the holy fathers:"

> "Whence," he says, "we, confirming what they did, have judged the aforesaid Flavian and Eusebius alien from all sacerdotal and episcopal dignity."

---

[w] Acta Conc. Eph. ii., read at Counc. of Chalcedon Act. i. Conc. iv. 1161. sqq. Col.

S. Flavian said, "I decline thee" [thy judgements]; the Roman deacon, "It is contradicted." The Bishops of the Robber-Council in different terms passed sentence upon S. Flavian and Eusebius, as having contravened the Canon of Ephesus and become subject to its penalties. Juvenal, Bishop of Jerusalem, who voted first, said,

> "Flavian and Eusebius have shewn themselves aliens from the priesthood and the episcopal band, who endeavoured to add to or diminish aught from the faith set forth in the holy Council of Nice, which the holy Œcumenic Synod, which met here of old in Ephesus, confirmed, so that those who should venture to add or diminish should be alien from the priesthood, especially making such confusion."

Domnus of Antioch simply condemned them, as "not abiding in the holy Council of Nice and that here assembled." The rest followed in the same sense.

At the Council of Chalcedon, the judges and senate pronounced,

> "Since Flavian of pious memory and the most reverend Bishop Eusebius, from the investigation of what was done and decreed, and from the words of some of the chiefs of the then Synod, who owned that they erred and deposed them wrongly, having erred in nothing against the faith, are shewn to have been unjustly deposed, it is just, (if it seem good to our most divine and religious Lord,) that Dioscorus, Juvenal, Thalassius, Eusebius, Eustathius, Basil, [naming their several sees] who held power and rule in the said Synod, shall be subject to the same penalty from the holy Synod, so as to become alien from the episcopal dignity, all which follows being made known to the sacred head."

The Council of Chalcedon agreed to this by acclamation; the Bishops of Illyricum and those with them, who had been members of the Robber-Council, accepting it also, only saying, "we have all erred, let us all obtain pardon," asking for the deposed Bishops also.

The Robber-Council, then, deposed S. Flavian and Eusebius of Dorylæum, upon the interpretation of the Canon of the first Council of Ephesus, that it forbade, upon pain of deposition, to add or diminish ought to or from the faith, laid down till then: the Council of Chalcedon deposed those who had so acted, as having judged unjustly.

It is strange that an interpretation of the Canon of the 1st Council of Ephesus, which was abused by the Robber-Council to the deposition of S. Flavian, and for which deposition the heads of that Robber-Council were themselves pronounced liable to the same penalty, should still be held valid. The Robber-Council decided in the interests of its President, Dioscorus, and his heresy. But the heresy was kept out of sight. The Robber-Council put forward simply the Canon of Ephesus, with the interpretation, that it forbade all additions beyond the very words of the Creed; it condemned Flavian on this ground only, and deposed him in conformity with the Canon so interpreted. If their interpretation of the Canon was right, the deposition was right. But those of the Robber-Council, who were present at the Council of Chalcedon, confessed that they had been wrong; the judges and senate at that Council pronounced the chiefs of them "subject to the same penalty from the synod;" the Council approved of that decision.

Protestants may reject consistently the authority of all Councils; but on what ground any who accept their authority can insist on their own private interpretation of a Canon of one Council, against the authority of another General Council which rejected that interpretation, I see not.

The Council of Chalcedon, which is appealed to as rëenacting the Canon of Ephesus, in the sense which Dioscorus attributed to it, had to defend S. Leo against its having that meaning, attributed to it by the Eutychians.

The Allocution of the Council of Chalcedon to the Emperor Marcian, is a defence of S. Leo:

> "[x] That the most holy Archbishop wrote the letter to Flavian, Archbishop of the royal city of Constantinople, now among the saints, not innovating any thing against the faith in Nicæa, but following the holy fathers, who also afterwards in like way refuted the heresies which sprang up from time to time after the great Synod of Nice."
>
> "Lest any one, declining the harmony of faith and trying to hide the confutation of his own deceit, should accuse the composing of that epistle as foreign and not legalised by the canons, saying that it was not meet that there should be any exposition of the faith, beside that of the fathers at Nice, the law of the Church advises that there should be one summary of teaching, that of the 318, which, as a common watchword from saints, we commit to those who are baptised for the security of their adoption as sons. But it is necessary to meet those who essay to pervert right doctrine, as to each of their productions, and to confront their devices in a fitting way. If all were satisfied with the recognised faith

[x] Conc. Chalc. P. iii. c. 1. Conc. iv. 1757. Col.

and did not innovate in the path of godliness, the Church would have no need to devise any thing in addition to the Creed for demonstration. But since many turn from the right way to the way of error, devising for themselves some new path to falsehood, it was necessary that we too should convert them by new statements of truth, and array refutations against their devices; not as if ever discovering something lacking to faith for godliness, but as devising what is expedient in regard to their novelties.

They then recite words of the Creed, "I believe in our One Lord Jesus Christ, the Son of God, of one Substance with the Father," and illustrate how it had been necessary to explain this.

S. Agatho, in his epistle to the Emperor at the vith General Council, insists on the transmission of the one faith undiminished, unaugmented.

"[y] Among men, whose lot is in the midst of heathen, and who gain their food very precariously by the labour of their hands, how could the full knowledge of Scripture be found, unless we keep in simplicity of heart and unhesitatingly, what has been canonically defined by the saints before us and by the five holy Councils, of the faith handed down by the fathers, ever using all prayers and zeal to hold one special thing, that nothing should be diminished, nothing changed or *added*, beside [z] what has been canonically defined, but the same things be guarded inviolate both in word and deed?"

Yet he proceeds to lay down the faith against Monothelism in distinct dogmatic terms,

"[a] Since we confess two natures, and two natural

---

[y] Conc. Const. iii. Act. iv. Ep. 1. Conc. vii. 655. Col.
[z] The Greek has the word of the Canon of Ephesus, παρά.
[a] Ib. 657, 660.

wills and two natural operations, in our one Lord Jesus Christ, we do not say that they are opposite or contrariant to one another (as they who err from the way of truth of the Apostolic tradition accuse us; far be such ungodliness from the heart of the faithful!), nor as if separate in two persons or hypostases; but we say that one and the same Lord Jesus Christ, as He has two natures, so He had in Himself two natural wills and operations, Divine and Human; that the Divine Will and Operation He hath from everlasting, common with His own Consubstantial Father, but the human, taken in time from us with our nature."

In like way the definition of the 2nd Council of Nice has,

"[b] We, having examined and considered with all accuracy, and following the mark of truth, neither subtract any thing, nor add, but guard thoroughly all of the Catholic Church undiminished, and following the six holy œcumenical synods, and first of all, that which was gathered in the glorious metropolis of Nice, and moreover, after it, in the God-defended royal city."

Then it rehearsed the Creed of Constantinople, and in brief accepted the 6 General Councils and the traditions writen or unwritten: and then it pronounced its decree about eikons.

Card. Julian produced all these instances in the Council of Florence[c]. Mark of Ephesus allowed that the Nestorian Creed was rejected by the Council of Ephesus, because it was contrary to the faith; that the Creed of Charisius, though differing in language and doctrinal statements, was admitted, as agreeing with the faith; but continued to argue, that the Canon, by its word παρὰ, prohibited any varia-

[b] Act. vii. Conc. viii. 1203, 1204.   [c] Sess. xi.

tion from the *terms* of the Creed although not differing in doctrine. At last, according to the Greek writer of the Acts, Mark summed up, "[d] not as disputing, but as wishing to put an end to the matter."

The same practice of presenting from time to time, as occasion required, a creed enlarged beyond that of Constantinople or other than it, has been continued in later times. Le Quien puts together the following instances,

"[e] In the 6th Council also, no one objecting, Peter of Nicomedia, Theodore, and other Bishops, Clerks and monks, who had embraced the Monothelite heresy, openly recited a Creed longer and fuller than the Nicene[f].

In the 7th Synod also, another was read written by Theodore of Jerusalem[g]: and again, Basil of Ancyra, and the other Bishops, who had embraced the errors of the Iconoclasts, again offered another[h], although the Canon of Ephesus pronounced, that 'it should not be lawful to offer to heretics, who wished to be converted to the Church, any other Creed than the Nicene.' In this same Synod, was read another profession of faith, which Tharasius had sent to the Patriarchs of the Eastern sees[i]. It contains the Nicene, or Constantinopolitan Creed, variously enlarged and interpolated. But of the Holy Spirit, it has specifically this: 'And in the Holy Spirit, the Lord, the Giver of Life, which proceedeth from the Father through the Son.' But since the Greeks at the Council of Florence said, that these were individual, not common, formulæ of faith, here are others, which are plainly common and solemn, which are contained in their own rituals. They do not

---

[d] Conc. Flor. Sess. xv. p. 216.
[e] Diss. Dam. n. 37. [f] Sext. Syn. Gen. Act. 10.
[g] Conc. Nic. ii. Act. 3. [h] Ib. Act. 1. [i] Ib. Act. 3.

baptize a Hebrew or Jew, until he have pronounced a profession of Christian Faith, altogether different from the Creed of Constantinople, as may be seen in the Euchologion ʲ. In the consecration of a Bishop, the Bishop elect is first bidden to recite the Creed of Constantinople; and then, as if this did not suffice, a 2nd and a 3rd are demanded of him; of which the last contains that aforesaid symbol, intermingled with various declarations. Nay, Photius himself is pointed out to be the author of this interpolated symbol ᵏ. I pass by other formulæ, which the Greeks have framed for those who return to the Church from divers heresies or sects, although the terms of the Canon of Ephesus are, that 'it is unlawful to propose any other faith to those who wish to be converted to the Church, from heathenism, or Judaism, or any heresy whatever.' Either then, let them acknowledge themselves guilty of violating this sanction, or let them cease to speak against the Latins for adding to the Creed one little declaration."

The original objection, however, was not to the addition to the Creed; for although the Council of Toledo was prior in time, the accession (of which the Bishops of the Council themselves were not conscious) was not known. At what time, or under what influence the language " and from the Son," which was used so freely by S. Epiphanius and S. Cyril, as well as occasionally by other Greek fathers, came to be disused in the East, we know not. Yet in the 7th century, it furnished a pretext for those who wished to pick a quarrel with the West. The Monothelites, having been condemned by the first Lateran Council under Martin I, A.D. 649, objected to the statement that the Holy Spirit pro-

ʲ p. 844.
ᵏ In the codex Cæsareus, mentioned by Lambecius, L. vii. cod. 77.

ceeded from the Son also. They had come, as did so many Greeks afterwards [1], to deny the Eternal Procession of God the Holy Ghost through the Son, and limited words, by which the fathers declared it, to His temporal mission after our Lord's Ascension[m]. This denial of the faith they accompanied with the blasphemy of alleging it to be an error, that "[n] the Lord was free, as Man, from original sin." S. Maximus the Confessor (himself a Constantinopolitan until the outburst of the Monothelite heresy, and the friend of Pope Martin,) writes that the Romans

> "[n] produced consonant testimonies of the Latin fathers and of Cyril of Alexandria out of his sacred work on the holy Evangelist John, from which they shewed that they did not make the Son the Cause of the Holy Spirit. For they knew that the Father

[1] "All who, from the time of Cerularius to John Beccus" (who was won to the Latin side by Nicephorus Blemmidas, and was Patriarch A.D. 1272,) accordingly above 200 years, "wrote in behalf of the schism, with one consent maintained no Procession of the Holy Spirit from the Father through the Son, except that temporal manifestation or granting of spiritual gifts." Le Quien p. xxiii. xxiv. He instances Michael Psellus who explained "the Procession through the Son" that He was "imparted by Him and partaken by all creation;" Nicetas of Nicomedia, "given through the Son to sanctify the creature, or, according to others, because He passed through the Son to sanctify men;" perhaps another Bishop of Nicomedia, "was sent or given through the Son:" Andronicus Camaterus explained even S. Cyril's, that He "was the own Spirit of the Son and in Him and *from Him*," to be "not of His procession, but of His mission, gift or supply." Ib.

[m] The Monothelite, Macarius of Antioch, glossed, "the Holy Spirit Who proceedeth from the Father and shone forth through the Son," with the words "viz, to men." vi[th] Gen. Council, Act. 8. Conc. vii. 772. Col., whereas in the Fathers all the like words are used of the eternal Procession. See Pet. de Trin. vii. 10.

[n] Ep. ad Marin. Opp. ii. 70.

is the one Cause of Son and Spirit; of the One, according to Generation; of the Other, according to Procession; but (they used it) to convey that the One came through the Other, and to shew thereby the community of Substance and invariableness."

S. Maximus calls the objection "a subterfuge" of the adversaries (Monothelites). Anastasius, who was long Apocrisiarius of the Roman see at Constantinople, writes about A.D. 754,

"° We have besides translated from the Epistle of S. Maximus to Marinus Presbyter, the details concerning the Procession of the Holy Spirit, where he implies that the Greeks falsely except against us, since we do not say that the Son is the Cause or Principle of the Holy Spirit, as they imagine, but, knowing the Oneness of Substance of Father and Son, we confess that, as He proceeds from the Father, so He proceeds from the Son, understanding by the Emission, the Procession. Herein he interprets piously, and instructs to peace those who know both languages; in that he teaches both us and the Greeks, that in one way the Holy Spirit proceedeth, in another He doth not proceed from the Son, signifying the difficulty of expressing in one language the specialty of the other. By the like pious interpretation S. Athanasius formerly united Easterns and Westerns, when disagreeing about the word Hypostasis or Person, teaching that both believed and held the same truth, although, on account of the difference of language, they confessed it differently, and were angrily and idly contending with each other."

It is to be hoped that Photius, with his great

° Epist. ad Joann. Diac. This quotation by Anastasius (as Le Quien observes p. v.) authenticates beyond question the genuineness of the passage of S. Maximus, which some questioned.

learning, did not know of this, when, with such terrible force, he threw it into the balance, as a makeweight for his schism. "He, one and the same," says a writer on the Greek side [p], "both set himself to divide the Churches, using the difference of doctrine as a colour, and again made the agreement of the Churches the price of his private advantage."

iii. 2. In regard to the doctrinal propositions accepted at the Bonn Conference, I cannot but fear that Dr. Döllinger has embarrassed himself, by trying to extract an adequate confession of our faith out of S. John of Damascus, a writer who was, I conclude, unacquainted with the earlier Greek fathers, whose language he rejects, and who certainly knew nothing of our Latin fathers, and so nothing of the uniform agreement of Western expression of doctrine. As we have now such large knowledge of the Greek fathers, it would, I think, have been safer in the long run, if Dr. Döllinger had formed his propositions upon the whole range of the Greek fathers, instead of limiting himself to this one later writer, who was severed from the rich resources of the earlier by the Mohammedan desolation.

S. John of Damascus held, I doubt not, the same faith as the fathers, although he distinctly rejects their language without any qualification. In one place, he speaks only of the language, used currently in his time.

> "[q] We say, both that the Holy Spirit is from the Father, and we call Him the Spirit of the Father; but we do not say that the Spirit is from ($ἐκ$) the Son, but we call Him the Spirit of the Son."

[p] G. Scholarius de process. Sp. S. cont. Lat. in Le Quien p. xi.
[q] de fide orthod. i. 8.

In another place, he repeats this denial in a more doctrinal form,

> "[r] The Holy Spirit is not the Son of the Father, but the Spirit of the Father, as going forth *out of* the Father; and the Spirit of the Son, not as *out of* Him, but as proceeding through Him *out of* the Father; for the Father is the only Author."

and again [s],

> "The Holy Ghost is a Personal Production and Procession; from the Father and belonging to the Son, but not *out of* (ἐξ) the Son, as being the Spirit of the mouth of God, declaratory of the Son."

This language appeared to S. Thomas Aquinas erroneous, and, although I think with Le Quien, that it may be explained consistently with truth, I the more regret that the only doctrinal statement framed at Bonn with regard to the Procession of God the Holy Ghost from the Son is one, which, in its obvious sense, denies it. The Bonn proposition stands without any explanation; "the Holy Ghost goes *not* forth out of the Son;" and then assigns the ground, why He does not so go forth; "because there is in the Godhead but one Beginning &c." In the first Proposition, it was said, "The Holy Ghost goeth forth out of the Father, *as* the Beginning &c. In the second it is not said, "The Holy Ghost goeth not forth out of the Son, *as* a Beginning or Cause," which would have had the same meaning, as the denial so often made by the Westerns, that there are two Principles in the Godhead.

I wish then that the proposition had been framed, as you, who are not responsible for it, would wish

[r] Ib. 12.   [s] See ab. p. 9.

to interpret it, but in a sense which the words, as they stand, could not bear.

> "The Holy Ghost goes not forth out of the Son, (ἐκ τοῦ υἱοῦ,) as a distinct source of Being, because there is in the Godhead but one Beginning (ἀρχή), one cause (αἰτία)."

or (as I said just now)

> "The Holy Ghost goes not forth out of the Son as a Beginning or Primary Cause."

You proposed to deny this again, but Dr. Döllinger thought that "the statement is scarcely likely to content the Orientals." This, I think, can hardly be explained in any other sense, than that the Orientals would not be content to leave us in possession of any equivalent to the ἐκ, even although we should explain it, so as to exempt it from the imputation, which they have been taught from Photius to attach to it. The rejection however of the ἐκ is absolute. "The Holy Ghost goes not forth out of the Son, ἐκ τοῦ υἱοῦ; *because* there is in the Godhead but one Beginning, one Cause &c." This is as much as to say, that God the Holy Ghost cannot be said *in any sense* to proceed 'from the Son,' because, in whatever way this might be affirmed, it would involve, that there was more than one Beginning in the Godhead.

This is equivalent to what Mark of Ephesus said at the Council of Florence, which came to this, that, let the Latins explain how they would, so long as they retained the word "from," they *must* mean, "as from a distinct source;" in other words, "they must deny in their hearts what they acknowledged with their lips."

This makes another of the Bonn propositions ambiguous at best, even if it is not construed as involving a rejection of our hereditary way of confessing the faith.

> "[†] We reject every proposition, and every mode of expression, in which any acknowledgement of two principles or ἀρχαί or αἰτίαι in the Trinity *may be* contained."

For it was the calumny of Photius, that it *was* contained in the Latin confession, "from the Father and the Son." The Greeks then, as long as they believe his calumny, must suppose, not only that it *may be*, but that it *is*, so contained; and we, by accepting this proposition, would seem to be disowning our one confession of the faith, the *Filioque*. It looks to me, as if this "introductory proposition," was meant to be preparatory to the rejection of the ἐκ.

It might have been said more simply,

> "We deny the supposition of two principles in the Trinity, as contrary to our belief in the Unity of God."

This would have explained to the Easterns what we do *not* mean, although it would not have said, what we do mean and believe. This would have been more nearly expressed, had the doctrine of S. John of Damascus been expressed more fully in the 3rd Proposition;

> "The Holy Ghost goes forth out of the Father through the Son [*eternally*]."

For S. John of Damascus, in two of the places alleged, is distinctly speaking of the Eternal Pro-

[†] Prop. iv.

cession. In answer to the Manichæan objection, "Was not thy God changed, when He begat a Son and possessed a Spirit?" he says,

> "[u] By no means. For I do not say, that, not being before Father, He afterwards became Father; but *He ever was,* having from (ἐξ) Himself His own Word, and from Him through His Word His Spirit Proceeding."

In a second place,

> "[v] The Father is Father and not Son. For He is from none. The Son is Son, from the Father, and not Father, that the Father may be One. The Holy Spirit, Holy Spirit going forth from the Father through the Son and Word, *but not after the manner of a Son.*"

Since then the relation of the Son to the Father, of which he is speaking, is eternal, so is also that relation of the Holy Spirit to the Father *through* the Son, which he contrasts with that of the Son; "not after the manner of a Son."

I regret that, in the Greek extracts from S. John of Damascus, those expressions were omitted, which marked that he was speaking of the Eternal Procession and Being of God the Holy Ghost, whereas the last, which is the only unambiguous statement, relates only to the temporal.

That this *was* his meaning, appears also from the saying, which is quoted in the 4th of the Bonn propositions, though too abstract, and too unauthorised by Holy Scripture, I think, for a dogmatic proposition, to be proposed for general acceptance.

[u] c. Manich. Dial. n. 5. Opp. T. i. pp. 431, 432.
[v] de hymno trisagio fin. Opp. i. 497.

"ʷ The Son is the image (εἰκών) of the Father, and the Spirit of the Son."

For this (which is the language also of S. Athanasius S. Basil and S. Cyril of Alexandria) although a statement rather requiring explanation and proof, than furnishing either, implies an eternal relation of God the Holy Ghost to the Son, as of the Son to the Father.

S. John Damascene says also in the same place,

"ˣ The Holy Spirit is united through the Son to the Father," and, "The Holy Spirit also is God, a sanctifying Power, Personal, proceeding indivisibly from the Father, and resting *in* the Son, of one substance with the Father and the Son."

This is the identical teaching of S. Gregory the Great;

"ʸ It is manifest that the Paraclete Spirit proceedeth from the Father, and abideth *in* the Son."
"ᶻ Unlike the way in which He dwelleth in the Saints, the Spirit abideth *in* the Son, from Whom by nature He never departeth."

And S. Andrew of Crete:

"ᵃ For the Father cannot be contemplated except in the Son, or the Son, except in the Father, save in the Holy Ghost, Who proceedeth from the Father, but dwells essentially and reposes *in* the Son, as being Consubstantial, and co-enthroned and of like dignity."

Vigilius Tapsensis states the Procession from God the Son as a consequence of this,

"ᵇ We have proved by many testimonies of the

ʷ de fid. orthod. i. 13. p. 151.   ˣ Dial. ii. 38. Gr. Transl. See Le Quien Diss. Dam. i. 22. p. xi.   ʸ Mor. iii. n. 22.
ᶻ Ib.   ᵃ In Transfig. p. 52, 53. Comb.
ᵇ De Trin. c. xi. Bibl. Patr. viii. 795. Le Q. p. xii.

Scriptures, that He is the Spirit of the Son and that He abideth whole *in* the Son; and as He proceedeth from God the Father, so He proceedeth from the Son, that the whole Trinity may be believed to be one God."

If the belief of the present Greeks is the same as that of S. John Damascene, they could not except against our Western formula. Their forefathers listened to the calumnies of Photius, that the Westerns contradicted the Monarchia, which the Westerns always unvaryingly believed, and which never was questioned, except by some early Greek heretics. But this being believed, there cannot be the slightest difference between the Greek and Latin expressions of belief. This, as far as the Latins were concerned, was owned by one who became an enemy of the Council of Florence, George Scholarius, who draws out the Latin side very clearly, but leaves ambiguities in the Greek statement.

"[c] Since we Greeks heretofore thought, that the Latins affirmed, that the Holy Spirit proceedeth from the Father and the Son, as from two Principles and two Spirations, and moreover did not affirm that the Father was the principle and fountain of the whole Deity, viz. of the Son and the Holy Spirit, therefore we have abstained from their addition or unfolding in the Creed, and likewise from their Communion. But now we being collected into this sacred and Œcumenical Synod, by the singular grace of God, to bring about a holy union, after many questions and discussions had and ventilated, and very many testimonies being produced both from Holy Scripture and the holy doctors of

[c] Syrop. sect. 8. c. 17. Le Qu. p. xxvii. xxviii.

the Church, we the Latins profess, that we do not say that the Spirit proceedeth from the Father and the Son, meaning to exclude the Father from being Principle and Fount of the whole Godhead, viz. of the Son and the Holy Spirit, or as believing that the Son hath not from the Father, that the Holy Spirit proceedeth from the Son, or as setting forth that there are two principles or two productions of the Holy Spirit; but we confess that the Holy Spirit eternally emanateth from the Father and the Son as from one Principle and by one Production: in like way, we Greeks profess and believe that the Holy Spirit proceedeth from the Father, and is the own Spirit of the Son, and streameth forth from Him, and we profess and believed that He is poured forth by Both Substantially, viz. by the Father through the Son."

Scholarius shewed that he clearly understood the Latin doctrine, and his statement is a formal disowning of the imputations of Photius. His statement of the Greek doctrine is a remarkable contrast with his elaborate statement of the Latin. It consists only of unexplained sayings of some Greek fathers, capable by themselves of being understood without any reference to the Eternal Being of God, and perhaps the more so, as standing in contrast with the definite statements which he had put into the mouth of the Latins. On being asked to explain, Scholarius made no answer, and soon after left the Council. The Greeks answered, that the Westerns rejected the sayings of the Fathers. They were only asked, in what sense they used them; e.g. whether they still excepted against the 'addition,' whether they believed what they set forth as the Latin doctrine, as explained by themselves, and would be united in it; whether they understood the "pouring forth" to be from eternity, and to relate to Substance and Person; what they meant by "pouring forth," whether it meant the same as to "proceed," &c.

The Council adopted the statements of Scholarius, only leaving out what was ambiguous; and whatever the Greeks may think of the Council of Florence, any who wish to know our belief could not find it more carefully or precisely stated:

"[d] Seeing that in this holy Œcumenical Council, by the grace of Almighty God, we Latins and Greeks have come together for an holy union to be made between us, and have taken diligent care one with another, that that Article on the Procession of the Holy Ghost should be discussed with great care and diligent enquiry: testimonies too having been brought forward from the Divine Scriptures and full many authorities of holy Doctors Eastern and Western, some saying that the Holy Ghost proceeds from the Father and the Son, others from the Father through the Son, and all intending the same meaning under different words: We the Greeks have declared that what we say, that the Holy Ghost proceeds from the Father, we do not say with intent of excluding the Son: but, because we thought that the Latins said that the Holy Ghost is of the Father and the Son as of two Origins and two Spirations, we have abstained from saying that the Holy Ghost proceeds from the Father and the Son. And we the Latins affirm that what we say, that the Holy Ghost proceeds from the Father and the Son, we do not say in the sense of excluding the Father from being the Source of all Godhead,

[d] Conc. xviii. 1146. Col.

of the Son, that is, and the Holy Ghost: or that this, that the Holy Ghost proceeds from the Son, the Son hath not from the Father, or in the sense of affirming that there are two Sources or two Spirations, but we affirm that there is One sole Source and Only Breathing of the Holy Ghost, as heretofore we have asserted."

De Turrecremata even proposed to anathematise the heresy imputed to the Latins:

"[e] We follow the Apostolic See, we know that there is one Cause of the Son and the Holy Spirit, the Father...... Therefore the Roman Church doth not believe two Principles or two Causes, but One Principle and One Cause. But those who assert two Principles or two Causes we anathematise."

Any one, who wishes to understand our Western belief, not merely to except against it, should study these statements.

Pope Gregory X had, in and with the 2nd Council of Lyons (A.D. 1274), formally condemned any who should presume so to hold. Its first Canon set forth the Latin belief, which it declares to be the same as that of the Greek fathers:

"[f] We acknowledge, with a true and faithful profession, that the Holy Spirit proceeds eternally from the Father and the Son, not as from two Principles, but as from One Principle; not by two spirations but by one only spiration. This the most holy Roman Church, the mother and mistress of all faithful, has hitherto professed, preached, and taught: this it firmly holds, preaches, professes, and teaches: this is the irrefragable and true mind of orthodox fathers and doctors, Latins alike and Greeks. But since some, for ignorance of the aforesaid irrefrag-

[e] Le Qu. p. xxvii.   [f] Conc. xiv. 520. Col.

able truth, have fallen into divers errors, we, hoping to close the way against such errors, the sacred Council approving, condemn and reprobate all, who should presume to deny that the Holy Spirit proceeds eternally from the Father and the Son, or, with rash presumption, to assert, that the Holy Spirit proceeds from the Father and Son, as from two Principles and not as from One."

Amid the unhappy relations of East and West, and absence of intercourse, this declaration of a Council, in which 500 Bishops, 70 Abbots, and 1000 Prelates of inferior rank [g], as also Greek ambassadors were present, was forgotten as if it had never been made, and the old imputation, that the Latins held two Principles in the Godhead, was perpetuated.

Dr. Döllinger rightly insisted, that the Greeks attached to the Greek expression, ἐκπορεύεσθαι, a meaning, which we do not attach to our Western, 'proceed from.' He does not notice that they attach to it a meaning, which, by the force of the term, it has not. No one questions their right to ascribe to it, *for themselves*, what meaning they please. But ἐκπορεύεσθαι, in itself, only signifies to " proceed out of." It does not in itself signify " to proceed out of *as the original source of Being*." Nor have they any authority to blame us for not attaching that meaning to our Lord's word in Holy Scripture, or to our own substitute for it, to " proceed from." It does not lie in the word itself; nor has the Church authoritatively so limited its use. We do not speak Greek, nor require the Greeks to use our language. But we, Westerns, are the judges, what

[g] See Mansi on Raynald Ann. 1274. 1.

we mean by our own. In fact, as Dr. Döllinger pointed out, the case is parallel to the confusions, which there were, in the Arian period, about the word "Hypostasis," "Prosopon," and "Persona." When the misapprehension was cleared up, each went on using his own term. The Greeks, under the term ἐκ, have in their mind the relation of God the Father, as the original Source of Co-eternal Being, to the Son and the Holy Ghost; we, Westerns, under our term "from" (*a* or *ex*) have in our mind the relation of God the Holy Ghost to the other two Persons of the All-Holy Trinity, the Father and the Son. There is no contradiction between the statements, because we are speaking of different relations. They have only to accept our explanation, that, when we use the word "from," we are not thinking of the original Source of Divine Being. Nor is there any need of explaining that we hold the Monarchia. For the word "Father" in itself contains it.

iv. It were, I think, much to be desired that in the proximate conference at Bonn, those who take part in it, should consider more largely the range of teaching, in both Greek and Latin Fathers, in regard to the relation of God the Holy Ghost to the Father and the Son. East and West, in earliest times, used, each of them, language, which has since been adopted exclusively by the other.

At least, the "through the Son" is used in one place by Tertullian, and by S. Hilary; "from the Father and the Son" was used by several fathers of the Eastern Church.

Controversialists seem strangely to ignore the truth that there is Co-eternal order in the existence of the Three Divine Persons. Those who deny the Eternal Procession of God the Holy Ghost "from the Father *and* the Son" or "from the Father *through* the Son," do in fact deny any order in the existence of God, or relation of all the Divine Persons to Each Other. They acknowledge a relation of God the Son and God the Holy Ghost to God the Father, but deny their relation to Each Other. The Father is, in these representations, the One Source of Being, but dividing (so to speak) into two streams of Being, which have no relation to each other, except the oneness of their source.

The relation of the Three Divine Persons, Father, Son, and Holy Ghost, is laid down for us by our Lord in the Baptismal formula, nor may we depart from it. "[h] For we must be baptized, as we have received; and believe, as we are baptized; and glorify, as we have believed, Father Son and Holy Ghost." The order of the Co-eternal Three must be, as Themselves, co-eternal. S. Basil says [i],

> "The Holy Spirit is co-numbered with the Father and the Son, because also He is above creation. And He is placed, as we are also taught in the Gospel by the Lord, saying, 'go, baptize in the name of the Father and the Son and the Holy Spirit;' but he who places Him before the Son, or saith that He is elder than the Father, contraveneth the ordaining of God, and is alien from sound faith, not guarding the doxology as we have received...... So that innovation as to the order is an annulling of the very existence, and a denial of the whole faith. For it is alike ungodly to bring down the Spirit to the

---

[h] S. Basil Ep. 125. n. 3. Opp. iii. 216.
[i] Id. Ep. 52 ad Canon. n. 4. Opp. iii. 146. Petav. de Trin. vii. 6. 3.

creation, or to place It above Son or Father, either as to time or order."

"j The Spirit is co-pronounced with the Lord, as is the Son with the Father. For the name of Father and Son and Holy Ghost is spoken in the like way. As then the Son is to the Father, so the Spirit is to the Son, according to the order of the word delivered in Baptism. But if the Spirit is conjoined with the Son, and the Son with the Father, it is plain that the Spirit also is [conjoined] with the Father."

Both ways of speaking, "from the Father *and* the Son," and "from the Father *through* the Son," contained the same truth as to the existence of the Divine Persons; that the Father, as the One Source of Being, everlastingly communicates Himself to the Son, in that way called Generation, and that that Being flows on eternally to the Holy Spirit, being derived originally from the Father, but issuing to the Holy Ghost from Both, the Father and the Son, as One. S. Gregory of Nyssa, having met the objection, that, "if we believe God the Son to be Eternal, we should also believe Him to be Ingenerate or Unoriginate," by saying that "He ever co-exists with the ever-existing Father, united by Generation with the Ingenerateness of the Father;" says,

"k So also we speak concerning the Holy Spirit also, the difference being only in the Order of Being. For as the Son is conjoined with the Father, and deriving His Being from Him, is in no way posterior to Him in Being, so again the Holy Spirit also cohereth to the Son, Who in thought only is conceived as prior, according to the ground of the cause, to

j Id. de Sp. S. c. 17. n. 43. Opp. iii. 36. Ib.
k S. Greg. Nyss. c. Eunom. i. fin. Opp. ii. 428. Pet. vii. 3. 3.

the Hypostasis of the Spirit; for extensions of time have no place in the life before all time, so that, with the exception of the ground of the cause, in nothing does the Holy Trinity differ in Itself."

In this clause, κατὰ τὸν τῆς αἰτίας λόγον, S. Gregory seems to me to attribute a subordinate causation to God the Son, that He is, conjointly with the Father, the Cause of the Holy Spirit. For God the Father giveth all which He is to the Son, except being the Father. He gives to Him then the being, with Himself, the Cause of the Holy Spirit. Otherwise, since, according to S. Gregory, there is no other difference in the Holy Trinity, then (as Petavius argues) there would be none between the Son and the Holy Spirit. But this does not, in S. Gregory's mind, interfere with the belief that God the Father is the Primal Cause, as he says,

"[1] While confessing the unvaryingness of the Nature, we do not deny the difference of 'cause' and 'caused,' wherein alone we understand that the One is distinguished from the Other, that we believe that the One is the Cause, the Other from the Cause; and in that which is from the Cause again we perceive another difference. For the One exists immediately from the First, the Other *through* Him Who exists immediately from the First: so that the being Only-Begotten remains unambiguously as belonging to the Son, without having any doubt that the Spirit is from the Father, the intermediateness of the Son both preserving to Him the being Only-Begotten, and not excluding the Spirit from the natural relation to the Father. But in speaking of 'Cause' and 'from Cause,' we do not by these forms designate nature (for one would not speak

[1] Id. Ep. ad Ablabium. T. iii. p. 27. Ib.

of 'Cause' and 'Nature' as the same); but we point out the difference in the mode of existence."

He sums up [m],

"Speaking of such distinction in the Holy Trinity, that we believe 'the Cause' and the 'from the Cause,' we can be no longer accused of confounding the Persons in the community of Nature. Since then the principle of causation distinguishes the Persons of the Holy Trinity, setting forth that the one is 'the Cause,' the other, 'from the Cause,' but the Divine Nature is, amid every conception, understood to be immutable and indivisible, therefore properly are One Godhead and One God, and all the God-beseeming names, singularly enunciated."

With a view to the full consideration which I hope the subject will receive, I will set down first, what passages I have been able to collect, in which Greek fathers speak of the Procession of the Holy Ghost "*through*" the Son, meaning thereby His Eternal Procession; and in the same meaning, *from* the Father *and* the Son," as One.

To exhibit them in order of time.

No one could take Origen as an accurate exponent of the doctrine of the Holy Trinity. He needs to be explained, and does not explain. But, if capable of explanation, he may illustrate the language of others. Thus, he may be understood in a true sense, where he says,

"[n] We, being persuaded that there are Three Persons, the Father and the Son and the Holy Ghost, and believing that there is nothing else unoriginate but the Father, embrace, as most pious and true, that, of all things which have their being through

[m] Ib. p. 28.   [n] in S. Joan. T. ii. n. 6. Opp. iv. 61. de la Rue.

the Word, the Holy Spirit is more honourable than all, and in order, than all which have their being from the Father through Christ. And perhaps this is the cause why He is not called Son, the Only-Begotten Alone being by Nature Son from the beginning, of Whom the Holy Spirit seemed to have need, ministering to His Person, not only that He should be wise and reasoning and just, and all whatsoever we ought to think that He is by participation of those aforesaid conceptions of Christ."

Hard as this language is, perhaps (as it has been observed) it may mean, "that the Son only is and is called the Son, the Holy Ghost is not nor is called Son, because He is not immediately from the Father but through the Son °."

Origen's disciple, S. Dionysius of Alexandria, uses the same word *through* of the eternal Being of the Spirit,

"ᵖ Each of the Names, which I mentioned, is inseparable and inseverable from the next. I said 'Father' and, before I add 'the Son,' I have signified Him also in the Father. I added 'the Son :' if I had not before named 'the Father,' He would any how have been anticipated in the Son. I added 'the Holy Spirit,' but subjoined at the same time both *from* Whom and *through* Whom He proceeded (ἥκεν). But these do not know that neither can 'the Father,' as being 'the Father,' be alien from 'the Son,' for the Name is fore-beginning (προκαταρκτικὸν), nor is 'the Son' separable from 'the Father,' for the appellation 'Father' shews the community [of Nature]; and Theirs (ἐν ταῖς χερσὶν αὐτῶν) is the Spirit, Who cannot be without Him Who sendeth or Him Who beareth Him. How then can they

---

° Huet, quoted on Origen, l. c.
ᵖ S. Athan. de sent. Dionysii n. 17. Opp. i. 255. Ben.

who use these names, think that they are wholly severed and divided from One Another?"

and shortly after he adds,

"So then we both expand the indivisible Unity into the Trinity, and again sum up the Trinity, which cannot be lessened, into the Unity."

S. Athanasius himself adopts this language of S. Dionysius,

"ᑫ Before us and all creation the Word was and is Wisdom of the Father. And the Holy Spirit, being a Procession from the Father, is ever with (ἐστιν ἐν ταῖς χερσὶ) the Father Who sendeth and the Son Who beareth Him, through Whom He filled all things."

S. Athanasius sets forth the faith as to the Holy Spirit, as that "ʳ tradition which had been from the first, the teaching and faith of the Catholic Church, which the Lord gave, the Apostles preached, the fathers kept." He sums up,

"ˢ It is shewn harmoniously from the Holy Scriptures, that the Holy Spirit is not a creature, but the *very own* (ἴδιον) *of the Word and of the Godhead of the Father.* For thus is the teaching of the Saints gathered into one as to the Holy and Indivisible Trinity, and this is the one faith of the Catholic Church."

He argues the Divinity of God the Holy Ghost from His relation to the Son,

"ᵗ If on account of the unity of the Word with the Father, they will not that the Son Himself should

---

ᑫ Expos. Fid. end. Opp. i. 102.

ʳ Ep. i. ad Serap. n. 28. Opp. i. 676. Ben. Petav. Præf. in Theol. Dogm. T. ii. p. 6.

ˢ Ib. n. 32. p. 681.   ᵗ Ib. n. 2. p. 647. Ben.

be one of created things, but think Him, what He is in truth, the Creator of things made, why do they call the Holy Ghost a creature, Who hath the same oneness with the Son, which the Son hath with the Father?" And, "ᵘThe Son saith, 'what I have heard from the Father, the same I speak unto the world:' but the Spirit taketh from the Son. He saith, 'He shall take of Mine, and shall shew it unto you.' And the Son came in the Father's Name; but 'the Holy Ghost,' saith the Son, 'which the Father shall send in My Name.' Since then the Spirit hath the same order and nature to the Son, as the Son hath to the Father, how shall he who calleth the Spirit a creature, not, of necessity, think the same as to the Son?"

"ᵛThe Spirit then is not one of created things, but rather is shewn to be the very own ($ἴδιον$) Spirit of the Son and not alien from God.—But if the Son, since He is out of ($ἐκ$) God, is the very own of His substance ($ἴδιος\ τῆς\ οὐσίας\ αὐτοῦ$), it is of necessity that the Spirit which is said to be of ($ἐκ$) God is the very own (Spirit) of the Son according to His Essence ($ἴδιον\ εἶναι\ κατ'\ οὐσίαν\ τοῦ\ υἱοῦ$)." "ʷThe Spirit not being a creature, but united with the Son, as the Son is united with the Father."

"ˣSuch special relation as we know the Son hath to the Father, such we shall find that the Spirit hath to the Son."

This language, that the Holy Ghost is "the very own of the Son according to His Essence," is the stronger, because (as Petavius argues) S. Athanasius uses the very same of the relation of the Son to the Father;

ᵘ S. Ath. Ep. i. ad Serap. n. 20, 21. p. 669.
ᵛ Ib. n. 25. p. 673. Ben. Pet. vii. 4. 8.
ʷ Ib. n. 31. p. 679. Ben.
ˣ Id. Ep. 3 ad Serap. p. 691. Ben. Petav. ib. p. 384.

"ʸ Since the Word is the very own of the substance of God by nature (ἴδιος φύσει τῆς οὐσίας τοῦ θεοῦ) and is *of* (ἐκ) Him and *in* Him." "The true Son is by nature the real Son of the Father, the very own of His Essence, Only-begotten Wisdom." "The Word, then, is not a creature, but, alone, very own of the Father." "Not alien, but the very own of the essence of the Father."

Guarding then that "the Spirit is *in* Christ, as the Son is *in* the Father," "that the Spirit is in us, which is *in* His Word, which is *in* the Father," S. Athanasius uses this same word *through*, shewing at the same time, that he uses it of His eternal mode of Being.

"ᶻ The Spirit is not external to the Word, but being *in* the Word is *through* Him in God" (ἐν τῷ λόγῳ ὂν, ἐν τῷ θεῷ δι' αὐτοῦ ἐστιν). "ᵃ Since the Spirit is *in* the Word, it were plain that the Spirit is *in* (ἐν) God also *through* (διὰ) the Word."

So since the Father and the Son are absolutely one, and the Son is *in* the Father (as He Himself saith) as the Father is in the Son, he hesitates not to say the Son is, in the Father, the Fountain of the Holy Spirit.

"ᵇ Wherefore David singing to God, saith, 'For with (παρὰ) Thee is the well of life, in Thy light we shall see light.' For he knew that the Son, being with (παρὰ) the Father, is the Fountain of the Holy Spirit."

G. Pachymeres (a Byzantine historian who takes strongly the Greek side) relates, that among other

---

ʸ Orat. c. Ar. ii. n. 31. Petav. p. 694. Ben. Pet. vii. 6. 5.   ᶻ Ep. iii. ad Serap. n. 5. ᵃ Ib. n. 6. p. 695.
ᵇ de Incarn. et cont. Arian. n. 9. T. 1. p. 877.

passages, the Patriarch John Beccus was impressed by "*e* finding Athanasius say,

> that it was impossible in the order of the Trinity that the Spirit should be known, not processionally inexisting (προοδικῶς) but creaturely, as they say."

S. Basil in like way, uses the word *through* of the Eternal Being of God the Holy Ghost,

> "*d* One also is the Holy Spirit, which also is singularly enunciated, being united *through* the One Son with the One Father."

S. Basil uses this word *through* in both ways, ascending from the Holy Spirit to the Father or beginning from the Father.

> "*e* The way of the knowledge of God is from One Spirit *through* the One Son to the One Father; and conversely, natural goodness and natural sanctification and the royal dignity cometh from the Father *through* the Only-begotten to the Spirit."

And, in answer to the question, "why the Spirit was not the son of the Son,"

> "Not that He is not of (ἐκ) God through (δἰ) the Son, but lest the Trinity should be thought an endless number, being suspected to have sons from sons, as among mén."

The question, as well as the answer, implies the belief in the eternal relation of the Holy Spirit to the Son; for without this belief it could not have arisen, as Bessarion argued, who alleged the passage in the Council of Florence *f*.

c Pachymeres T. ii. p. 29 Bonn.   *d* De Sp. S. c. 18.
e Id. Ib. n. 47. in Petav. vii. 6. 5.   *f* Orat. Dogm. c. 6.
in Conc. Flor. Sess. 25. Conc. T. 18. p. 424 ed. Col.

S. Gregory of Nyssa in like way,

"[g] We come from the Father *through* the Son to the Spirit."

And again, as quoted by Bessarion [h],

"The Spirit, being joined to the Father, as Uncreated, is again distinguished from Him, in that He is not Father, as He is. But from the conjunction with the Son, as being Unbegotten, and that He hath the cause of His being from God the Father, He is distinguished by the property that He is not from the Father as Only-Begotten, and that He appeareth *through* the same Son. And again, whereas the creation exists through the Only-Begotten, that the Spirit may not be thought to have any thing common with it, because It appeareth through the Son, the Spirit is distinguished from the creation, in that It is unalterable and unchangeable and needeth no goodness from without."

Bessarion again quoted S. Maximus [i];

"For the Holy Spirit, as He is by nature, according to substance, God the Father's, so is He the Son's according to Substance, proceeding substantially from the Father *through* the Son, ineffably Begotten."

On the other hand, S. Basil also expresses this relation of the Holy Spirit by the word *from* παρὰ; as Didymus his contemporary does *out of*, and S. Epiphanius (whose Creed so much resembles, in part, that adopted at Constantinople) uses *out of* (ἐκ) exclusively.

Didymus, the teacher of S. Jerome and Rufinus, in his work on the Holy Spirit, translated by

---

[g] c. Eunom. L. i. ed. Grets. ap. Pet. vii. 6. 5.
[h] c. Eunom. L. i. ap. Bess. p. 428.   [i] Bess. l. c.

S. Jerome, "ᵏexplaining the words of our Lord, He shall not speak from Himself," writes,

> "That is, not without Me and the Will of the Father, because He is inseparable from Mine and the Father's Will. For He is not *of* (ex) Himself, but *of* (ex) the Father and Me. For His very Being He hath *from* (a) the Father and Me."—" The Holy Spirit also, Who is the Spirit of truth and the Spirit of Wisdom, cannot, when the Son speaketh, hear what He knoweth not ; since The Spirit of Truth proceeding is that Very Being, which is brought forth *from* (a) the Son, i. e., proceeding from the Truth, the Paraclete issuing *from* (a) the Paraclete, God *from* (a) God."

And on the words " He shall glorify Me, because He shall take of Mine,"

> "¹ Here again, to 'take' is to be understood, so as to be in harmony with the Divine Nature. For as the Son, when He giveth, is not deprived of those things which He giveth, nor, with loss to Himself, imparteth to others, so also the Spirit doth not receive what He had not before. For if He receive what before He had not, when the gift is transferred to another, the Giver is emptied, ceasing to have what He giveth. As then above, when disputing of incorporeal natures, we understood, so now too we must know, that the Holy Spirit receiveth from the Son that which had been of His own Nature, and that this signifieth, not a giver and a receiver, but One Substance. Inasmuch as the Son is said to receive of the Father That, wherein He Himself subsists. For neither is the Son ought besides what is given to Him *from* (a) the Father, nor is the Sub-

---

ᵏ De Spiritu Sancto n. 34. translated by S. Jerome Opp. ii. 142. Vall. Pet. de Trin. vii. 3, 5.   ¹ Ib. n. 36, 37. p. 147.

stance of the Holy Spirit other, besides what is given Him by the Son."

S. Epiphanius no where uses the word "through" but always [ἐκ] "from" when speaking of the Eternal Being of the Holy Spirit. And these are no chance passages of S. Epiphanius, but passages in which he is carefully stating and guarding the truth as to the existence of the Holy Trinity. The first is against the heresy of Sabellius.

> "[m] For the Spirit ever is, with the Father and the Son, not in relation of brother with the Father, not begotten, not created, not brother of the Son, not grandson of the Father, but ever proceeding from the Father and receiving of the Son: not alien from Father and Son, but *from* (ἐκ) the same Essence, *from* (ἐκ) the same Godhead, *from* (ἐκ) the Father and the Son, with the Father and the Son, ever subsisting Holy Spirit, Divine Spirit, Spirit of glory, Spirit of Christ, Spirit of the Father. For it is *the Spirit of the Father, Who speaketh in you*, and *My Spirit standeth in the midst of you*, the Third in appellation, equal in Godhead, not alien from the Father and the Son, the Bond of the Trinity, the seal of the confession."

And in his elaborate exposition of the faith[n], which he partly embodies in his writing against "the blasphemers of the Holy Ghost[o];"

> "[p] The Holy Spirit ever is, not begotten &c., but *from* (ἐκ) the same essence of the Father and the Son, the Holy Spirit. For God is Spirit." "[q] He is the Spirit of the Son; not by any composition, (as in us, soul and body) but in the midst of the

---

[m] S. Epiph. Hær. lxii. n. 4.   [n] Ancorat. Opp. T. ii.
[o] Hær. lxxiv.   [p] Anc. n. 7.   [q] Ib. n. 8.

Father and the Son, *from* (ἐκ) the Father and the Son, the third in appellation." "[r] Whole God is Wisdom; so then the Son is Wisdom from Wisdom, in Whom are hidden all the treasures of wisdom. Whole God is Life; therefore the Son is Life from Life. For 'I am the way, the truth and the life.' But the Holy Spirit *from Both* (παρ' ἀμφοτέρων) is Spirit from Spirit; for God is Spirit."

"[s] But some one will say, Do we then say that there are two Sons? How then is He Only-begotten? But who art thou, who speakest against God? For since He calls Him Who is from Him, the Son, and That which *is from Both*, (τὸ παρ' ἀμφοτέρων) the Holy Spirit; which being conceived by the saints through faith alone, being lightful, lightgiving, have a lightful operation, and by the light of faith are in harmony with the Father Himself; hear thou, that the Father is Father of Him, Who is the True Son and wholly Light, and the Son is of True Father, Light of Light, (not, as things created or made, in title only) and the Holy Spirit is the Spirit of Truth, the third Light *from* (παρὰ) Father and Son." "[t] As there are many sons by adoption or calling, not in truth, because they have beginning and end, and are inclined to sin, so there are very many spirits by adoption or calling, although inclined to sin. But the Holy Spirit is Alone entitled *from* (ἀπὸ) the Father and the Son, the Spirit of Truth, and Spirit of God, and Spirit of Christ and Spirit of grace." "[u] If then He proceedeth *from* (παρὰ) the Father; and, the Lord saith, He shall take of Mine, then in the same way, in which no one knows the Father save the Son, nor the Son, save the Father, so, I dare to say, that no one knoweth the Spirit, save the Father and the Son,

---

[r] Anc. n. 70.   [s] Hær. lxxiv. n. 8.
[t] Anc. n. 72. filled up from Hær. lxxiv. n. 9.   [u] Ib. 73.

from (παρ') Whom He proceedeth and from Whom He taketh, and neither doth any one know the Son and the Father, save the Holy Spirit, Who truly glorifieth, Who teacheth all things, Who testifieth concerning the Son, Who is *from* (παρὰ) the Father and *of* (ἐκ) the Son." "[v] The Father then ever was, and the Spirit breatheth *from* (ἐκ) the Father and the Son, and neither is the Son created, nor is the Spirit created. But all things, after Father and Son and Holy Ghost, being created and made, once not being, came into being from Father Son and Holy Ghost through the Eternal Word, with the Eternal Father."

"[w] Since Christ from (ἐκ) the Father is believed to be God from (ἐκ) God and the Spirit is from (ἐκ) Christ or from (παρ') Both, as Christ saith, 'Who proceedeth (παρὰ) from the Father and He shall take of Mine.'"

S. Basil uses παρὰ in the same sense, to express that the Spirit has His eternal Being directly from the Son. Eunomius argued, that "he had received from the saints, that the Paraclete was the third in order and dignity," and therefore he inferred that He was "third also in nature." S. Basil answers[x],

"Was there ever man so bold, introducing novelties into divine doctrines? For what need is there,

---

[v] Ib. 75.   [w] Ib. 67.

[x] The passage was adduced by the Latins in the Council of Florence, from a MS. brought from Constantinople by Card. Nicolas Cusanus. The disputed reading was "in a parchment MS. 600 years before the Council of Florence, and before the commencement of the controversy as to the Procession of the Holy Spirit," and "other very old books, whose antiquity is such that any one would own that they are prior to the schism." John de Turrecremata at the Council and Manuel Calecas c. 10. in Petav. vii. 3. 16.

that if the Spirit is third in dignity and order, He should be in nature? For, may be, the word of godliness transmits to us, that He is second in dignity from the Son, having His Being *from* (παρ') Him, and receiving *from* (παρ') Him: but that He hath a third nature, we have neither learned from the Holy Scriptures, nor can it be inferred as consequent from the things aforesaid. For as the Son is second in order from the Father, because He is *from* (ἀπ') Him, and in dignity, because the Father is the Beginning and Cause of His Being, and because the approach and bringing near to God the Father is through Him, but He is in no wise second in nature, because the Godhead in Each is One; so also the Holy Spirit, although He is subordinate to the Son in order and dignity, (even if *we* granted this) would not therefore be of another nature."

Even S. Cyril of Jerusalem, who avoided the word Homoöusion, not to give offence, says:

"[y] There is One and the Same Spirit, which sanctifieth and subsisteth, and is ever co-present with the Father and the Son, not being spoken or breathed forth *from* the mouth and lips of the Father or the Son, not dispersed into the air, but subsisting."

Reserving, for the time, the abundant evidences from S. Cyril of Alexandria, there continue to be traces of the "from" among Greek writers till A.D. 600, 50 years before S. John Damascene.

A Sermon attributed by Photius to S. Chrysostome[z], and, it is thought by some, contemporary, has the words;

[y] S. Cyril Jer. Cat. 17. n. 5. p. 223. Oxf. Tr.
[z] Hom. de Incarn. Dom., quoted by Photius cod. 277, as S. Chry-

"Christ came to us; He gave us the Spirit which is of Him [a], and took our body."

Severian, Bishop of Gabala, a Syrian, the contemporary and enemy of S. Chrysostome, in a homily translated from the Armenian, and so under no Western influences, has the doxology;

"[b] To the Unbegotten God the Father, and the Son, Begotten from Him, and the Holy Spirit proceeding from their Essence."

Philo Carpathius was a younger contemporary of S. Epiphanius, and, it is said, much trusted by him. His words, as occurring in an allegorical interpretation, attest the use of the word "from," beyond the strict doctrinal writers.

"[c] The mouth of God the Father is the Son. Wherefore, since He too is God, equal by nature to the Father, He is called the Word; since whatever the Father willeth, He speaketh, createth, frameth and preserveth through the Son together with that Divine Spirit, Who proceedeth from (ἐκ) the Father and the Son."

Anastasius Sinaita, Patriarch of Antioch, A.D. 561, to whom all the Eastern Bishops so looked up, that, when urged by the Emperor Justinian to accept his formula, they answered, that they waited to know the mind of Anastasius and should follow him, used it repeatedly.

---

sostome's, placed among the "Dubia" by Savile T. v. Hom. 125., among the "Spuria" by Montfaucon T. viii. App. 213.

[a] τὸ ἐξ αὐτοῦ πνεῦμα. Photius of course leaves out the ἐξ. "Beccus and Calecas, Savile" and Montf. (App. 224.) "have it." Petav. de Trin. vii. 3. 19.   [b] Hom. i. fin. p. 17. ed. Aucher.

[c] Philo Carpath. Comm. in Cant. ap. Pet. vii. 3. 11.

"d Taking the property of the mouth as an illustration, we have expressed the mutual connection (ἀλληλουχίαν) of the Divine Persons through the analogy and likeness of the members. For thus the Holy Spirit is said both to be the Spirit of His mouth, i. e. of God, since the Only-Begotten is the Mouth; and again the Spirit going forth from (ἐξ) Him, and sent, not only from (παρὰ) the Father, but also from (παρὰ) the Son." "e The Lord, shewing that It [the Spirit] is out of Himself (αὐτὸ ἐξ ἑαυτοῦ ὑπάρχειν), said to His disciples, breathing upon them, Receive the Holy Ghost."

"f We call the Father of the Word, Mind, in Whom is the Word, with Whom is the Holy Spirit, entitled the Spirit of the mouth of God; for the mouth of the Father is the Son."

And again g,

"What need of more words? since He Himself, from Whom the Holy Spirit proceedeth, openly bears witness to the truth concerning Himself, Who knows Himself and what is in Himself; for, the Evangelist saith, 'He knew what was in man.'"

The martyrdom of S. Dionysius the Areopagite in Symeon Metaphrastes is doubtless from older materials. It gives additional evidence for the wide-spread use of the form in the East.

"h And my Christ is raised to the heavens and

d Anast. Sinait. de rect. dogm. L. i. de Trinitate § 21 in Gallandi Bibl. Vet. Pat. xii. 241 (the Greek cited by Georg. Metochit. in Leonis Allat. Scriptt. Orth. Græciæ, t. ii. 1013, and by Joan. Plusiadenus, ib. i. 633.) Pet. vii. 5. 10, and 3. 19.

e Ib. § 27. (the Greek cited by Const. Melit. de Proc. Spiritus Sanct. ubi supra ii. 854) ap. Pet. vii. 3. 19.   f Ib. § 12 (the Greek cited by Georg. Met. ubi supra ii. 1013.)   g de rect. dogm. iii. de Incarnat. fin. Gallandi Bibl. Patr. xii. 251.

h Sym. Metaphr. in Mart. S. Dionys. init. Opp. S. Dionys. ii. 190. Pet. vii. 3, 19.

returns to His Father's throne, and sendeth on the disciples the Spirit Who proceedeth from Himself, to lead aright the unbelieving nations."

The most remarkable instance of the continuance of the formula, "of the Son," at this period is our great Archbishop Theodore, himself a native of Tarsus, well-versed, as is shewn in his Penitential, in the usages of the Greek Church, with which he parallels or contrasts those of the West. He shews himself also familiar with the Greek fathers, and the East of his own day had such confidence in him, that the vith General Council waited for him. On Sept. 17 A.D. 680, not quite two months before the opening of the vith General Council, Nov. 7, A.D. 680, he presided over the Council of Hatfield, in which the Confession of faith was drawn up, which embodied the *Filioque*.

In it, it is declared ;

> "[i] We have expounded the right and orthodox faith, as our Lord Jesus Christ, Incarnate, delivered to His Apostles who saw Him in bodily presence, and heard His discourses, and delivered the Creed of the holy fathers: and in general all the sacred and universal Synods and the whole choir of the Catholic approved doctors of the Church [have delivered it.]"

" And then after a brief confession of faith in the Holy Trinity in Unity, and a recital of the first five General Councils, and of the Lateran Council of A.D. 649, it thus concludes :—

> "And we glorify our Lord Jesus Christ as they

---

[i] Bede iv. 17. quoted from Rev. G. Williams, The Orthodox Eastern Church, in " The Church and the age" 2nd. series p. 237.

glorified Him, adding nothing, taking away nothing: and we anathematize in heart and word whom they anathematized: we receive whom they received: glorifying God the Father without beginning, and His Only-Begotten Son, Begotten of the Father before the ages: and the Holy Ghost, proceeding from [ex] the Father and the Son, ineffably; as those holy Apostles, and prophets, and doctors, whom we above commemorated, have preached."

Where, it may be observed, they use the "adding nothing, taking away nothing," so often repeated from the Council of Ephesus. These also must have been persuaded, like the rest, that the "et Filio" was no "addition," since through the Unity of the Father and the Son, whereby the Son had all which the Father had, except being "the Father," it really lay in the words "from the Father."

To return to S. Cyril, as a library in himself.

S. Cyril of Alexandria, as he was well nigh the last of the Greek Fathers, so also he was one, who in his life and soon after his death was accounted the most weighty. President of the 3rd General Council, in his own name and that of Pope Celestine, two of his Epistles received the seal of that Council, and a third that of the Council of Chalcedon; in the Council of Chalcedon, holden a few years after his death, his name stands for the whole Council of Ephesus. Wonderful, for its dogmatic precision, as was the Tome of S. Leo, Bishop after Bishop declares that he received it, because it agreed with the exposition of the 318 holy fathers at Nice and 150 at Constantinople and the synodical Epistles of our most holy father Cyril, or the things done under him or his mind [j]. When doubts were entertained by Bishops of Illyricum and Palestine as to three passages of S. Leo, the difficulties were removed by the production of similar passages of S. Cyril [k].

In the 6th General Council passages from various works of his were cited against Monothelism [l]. Some thirty years after his death, Gennadius says of him, "[m] He made very many Homilies, which the Greek Bishops commit to memory and deliver."

The force of S. Cyril's language does not lie in the word "proceedeth," "is poured out from:" it is not dependent on any explanation of these words, whether he use them of His temporal or of His Eternal Procession. He does not (according to the gloss of the Emperor Theodosius Lascaris) say, that "God the Holy Ghost is the Spirit of the Son, because He sent Him on the Day of Pentecost." He says, that God the Son sent the Holy Spirit, being His own Spirit. Holy Scripture (the modern Greeks are compelled to acknowledge) calls the Holy Ghost, "the Spirit of the Son." The heresy of Nestorius occasioned S. Cyril to lay stress on the truth, that God the Holy Ghost is so, eternally. Nestorius, misbelieving our Lord to be mere man, maintained also that God the Holy Ghost dwelt in Him, or, again, that He gave It, as something external to Himself. S. Cyril insisted on the simple truth that God only could send God, and that God the Son could not be said truly to send the Holy Ghost,

[j] Conc. Chal. Act. iv.
[k] Ib. Act. ii. Conc. iv. 1238. after the reading of the Tome.
[l] Conc. Const. iii. Act. iv. pp. 681 sqq. 686 sq. Act. ix. p. 805. Act. x. 832. sqq. 839. sqq. 849.
[m] de virr. ill. c. 37. in S. Jer. Opp. ii. 973.

unless He bore an eternal relation to Him and essentially coexisted *in* Him. This he does with his usual fulness and precision of language, mainly using the preposition, ἐκ, *out of*. But he even adds to its force by the varied richness of his energetic and cumulative words. He calls Him "His very own and both in Him and out of [n] Him;" "both out of [n] Him and His very own;" "out of [n] Him and Essentially Inexistent in Him;" "being by nature in Him and out of [n] Him;" "He is by nature out of [n] Him," "He goeth forth out of [n] the Father and the Son," "is of the Substance of the Son;" "His very own Spirit, being the Spirit of His very own Essence and that of the Father;" "both out of [n] Him and in Him and His very own."

To exhibit some of these in detail;

In the Thesaurus, a work written with very great care and precision for the defence of the Faith as regards the Persons of the most Holy Trinity, under the title—

> "That the HOLY GHOST is out of (ἐκ) the Essence of the FATHER and the SON."

he says,

> "[o] Since therefore the Holy Ghost, coming to be in us, makes us conformed to God and *He goeth forth out of* (ἐκ) *the Father and the Son*, it is manifest that He is of the Divine Essence, being Essentially in It and going forth out of (ἐξ) It: even as the breath too which goeth out of (ἐξ) the mouth of man, though the illustration be poor and unworthy, for God will surpass all things."

A few pages before, he has another heading,

> "[p] That the Spirit is God and hath every way the

[n] ἐξ.   [o] Thes. Opp. v. i. 344. Ib. 345.   [p] Ib. 338,

same operation with the Son and is not alien from His Essence: also that, when God is said to dwell in us, it is the Spirit Who indwelleth."

Again,

"q Since Christ giveth laws, the Spirit, *as being by Nature in Him and out of* (ἐξ) *Him*, Himself too is Law-giver."

"r Since, when Christ reneweth us and transplaceth us into a new life, the Spirit is said to renew us as is sung in the Psalms to God, 'Thou shalt send forth Thy Spirit and they shall be created, and Thou shalt renew the face of the earth,' we must of necessity confess that the Spirit is of the Essence of the Son. For as being by Nature out of (ἐξ) Him and being sent by Him upon the creation, He worketh the renewal, being the Complement of the Holy Trinity. And if so, the Spirit is God and out of (ἐκ) God, and not a creature."

In the De Trinitate, a work whose scope is the same as that of the Thesaurus, but its execution more popular and less dialectic, and a work to which S. Cyril refers in his Commentary on S. John [s],

"t He sent us the Comforter out of (ἐκ) Heaven, through Whom and in Whom He is with us and dwelleth in us, not infusing into us an alien, but the own Spirit of His Essence and of that of His Father."

Again in reply to the words objected,

"u But they say that Christ said of Him, 'Out of

q Ib. 354.   r Ib. 358. The trifling variations from Aubert's text in these passages of the Thesaurus are from a Manuscript collated by my son in the Library of the Patriarch of Alexandria at Cairo. These passages are likewise exstant in a Syriac translation, in the MS. in the British Museum, Additional 14556, assigned by Dr. Wright to the sixth or seventh century, and so anterior to the controversy. The Alexandrian MS. contains the heading also.
    s pp. 87 C. 94 C. (pp. 100, 108 Ox. Tr.)
    t De Trinitate vii. Opp. v. i. 642.   u Ib. 657.

(ἐκ) Mine He shall receive and tell it to you.' They say therefore the Spirit is participant of the Son" [i.e. received from One external to Himself];

S. Cyril says,

"Not at all, far from it: for how should the Spirit, that is both out of (ἐξ) Him and in Him and His Very Own, partake of Him and be sanctified relatively, like those things which are without, and be by nature alien from Him Whose very Own He is said to be?"

In his great Synodic Epistle to Nestorius which has the sanction of the Œcumenical Council of Ephesus, S. Cyril says,

"ᵛFor even though the Spirit exists in His own Person, and is conceived of by Himself in that He is Spirit and not Son, yet is He not therefore alien from Him, for He is called 'the Spirit of Truth' and Christ is 'the Truth' and He is shed forth from (παρ') Him just as out of (ἐκ) God the Father."

In the explanation of his xii Chapters against Nestorius, which explanation was written at the request of the Council of Ephesus,

" ʷThe Only-Begotten Word of God, having become Man, remained thus too God, being all that the Father is, save only being the Father, and having *as His own* the Holy Ghost Which is *out of* (ἐκ) *Him and Essentially inexisting in Him.*

Again, in his work on the right faith, addressed to the Emperor Theodosius,

"ˣ He said, that He would baptize in fire and the

ᵛ S. Cyrilli Epistolae p. 74. Opp. v. ii.

ʷ Expl. cap. ix. Opp. vi. 154, 155. exstant also in Syriac in a MS. of the British Museum., Add. 12156, of the VIth century.

ˣ De Recta fide ad Theodosium Imperatorem. Opp. v. ii. 33. S. Cyril put forth this same treatise again in a more popular form

Holy Ghost, infusing into the baptized no Spirit alien to Himself, in manner of a servant and minister, but as being by Nature God with supremest authority, [He infused] the Spirit Which is out of (ἐξ) Him and His Very Own."

And in that to the Queens,

"ʸ The resurrection of Christ was not by the nature of the Body, although It was the very own Body of the Word Who was Begotten of God; but rather by that supreme power and Nature above creation, as in the Person of God the Father, out of (ἐξ) Whom the Son appeared equal and like in all things, and the Life-giving Spirit goeth forth through Both." (πρόεισι δι' ἀμφοῖν).

Or, out of controversy, in works or comments on Holy Scripture, it occurs as his natural every-day mode of expression,

"ᶻ Seeing He [the Holy Spirit] is the Spirit of God the Father and the Son also, Which is poured forth essentially out of (ἐκ) Both, i.e., out of (ἐκ) the Father through the Son."

"ᵃ For, in that the Son is God and of God by Nature (for He is truly begotten of God the Father) the Spirit is His Very Own and in Him and out of (ἐξ) Him, just as is conceived as to God the Father Himself.

And on S. John,

"ᵇ How shall we separate the Spirit from the Son, thus inexisting and essentially united, Who cometh

De Incarnatione Unigeniti, where the words again occur. Opp. v. i. 706. This is exstant in a Syriac version, attributed to Rabbula, Bishop of Edessa, a contemporary of S. Cyril.

ʸ de recta fide ad Reginas v. 51. Opp. v. 2. p. 172. Aub.

ᶻ De Ador. lib. i. Opp. i. 9.

ᵃ In Joel. ii. 28, 29. Opp. iii. 228. Aub. i. 337. Oxon.

ᵇ In Johann. lib. ii. t. iv. 126.

forth through Him and is by nature in Him, that It cannot be thought to be ought other than He, by reason both of identity of working and the very exact likeness of Nature? The blessed Paul having called That, which dwelleth in us, the Spirit of Christ, forthwith subjoined, "If Christ be in you," introducing entire likeness of the Son with the Spirit Who is His very own and is by nature poured forth from ($\pi\alpha\rho$') Him."

"[e] For since He is the Spirit of Christ and His mind, as it is written, being nought else but what He is, in regard to identity of nature, even though He be both conceived of and is individually existent, He knows all that is in Him. And Paul will be our witness, saying, "For who knoweth the things of man save man's spirit that is in him? Thus the things of God no one knoweth save the Spirit of God." Wherefore, as knowing what is in the counsel of the Only-begotten, He reporteth all things to us, not having the knowledge thereof from learning; that He may not seem to fill the rank of a minister and to transmit the words of another, but as His Spirit and knowing untaught all that belongeth to Him, out of Whom ($\dot{\epsilon}\xi$ $o\hat{v}$) and in Whom He is, He revealeth to the Saints the Divine mysteries; just as man's mind too, knowing all things that are in him, ministereth externally by uttered word the desires of the soul whose mind it is, seen and named in idea something different from it [the soul], not being other by nature, but as a part complemental of the whole, existing in it and believed to be born out of ($\dot{\epsilon}\xi$) it."

"[d] For see, see, calling the Paraclete 'the Spirit of truth,' i. e. of Himself, He says that He proceedeth from the Father. For as He is the Own Spirit of

[e] In Johann. L. x. p. 837.
[d] Ib. xv. 26. p. 910 B. ii. 607 ed. Oxon.

the Son by Nature, both existing in Him and going forth through Him (δι' αὐτοῦ προϊὸν) so of the Father also : and They, to Whom the Spirit is common, full surely Their Essence is not distinct."

" ᵉHaving foretold them that the Paraclete would come on them, He named Him 'the Spirit of truth,' i. e. of Himself; for He is the Truth. For that the disciples might know, that He promises them not the coming of an alien and foreign power, but that He will give Himself in another way, He calls the Paraclete 'the Spirit of Truth,' i. e. of Himself. For not as alien from the Essence of the Only-Begotten is the Holy Ghost conceived of, but He goeth forth Naturally thereout (πρόεισι ... ἐξ αὐτῆς), being nought else than *He* is, so far as identity of Nature, even though He be conceived of as existing in His own Person."

"ᶠFor for this cause He hath added, that 'He shall tell you the things also to come,' all but saying, This shall be a sign to you that the Spirit is full surely out of (ἐκ) My Essence and, is, so to speak, My Mind, that He shall tell you the things to come, even as *I* . . . . . . For not surely as *I* would He foretell the things to come, were He not surely both existent in Me and going forth through (δι') Me and of the same Essence with Me."

And on S. Luke,

"ᵍ Nor had He [the Word Incarnate] need of the Holy Ghost ; for the Spirit that proceedeth from God the Father is of Him and equal in Essence with Him."

The doctrine, as thus stated, is apart (as I said) from the *word* Procession, or the plea made by

ᵉ Ib. xvi. 13. p. 925 C.   ᶠ Ib. 926.
ᵍ Hom. in S. Lucam xi. Vol. 1. p. 46. Eng. Tr. These Homilies exist only in the Syriac.

modern Greeks, that the fathers, when they speak of the Procession of God the Holy Ghost from the Son, are speaking of the sending of the Holy Ghost under the Gospel. For the relation, of which S. Cyril speaks, belongs to the Divine Persons themselves. Although the Holy Spirit was given without measure to our Lord as Man, and He wrought His wonderful works by It, yet It was His very own Spirit as God, which was given to Him as Man; and He Himself gave It from Himself, as being eternally His own, "sending It forth out of His own fulness (ἐξ ἰδίου πληρώματος) even as the Father too doth." Thus then what is called the temporal Procession is a proof of the Eternal. The temporal Procession of the Holy Spirit from the Father and the Son is one and the same, because He is eternally by Nature the Spirit of Both. This is very clearly stated and illustrated in the 3 first chapters of his fourth Book against Nestorius.

> "[h] For He [the Word Incarnate] was confessedly glorified, when the Spirit wrought the Divine signs [our Lord's miracles on earth]: yet glorified, not as a God-clad man, gaining this from a Nature foreign to Him and above Him (as we too do) but rather as using His own Spirit, for He was God by Nature, and not alien to Him is His Spirit . . . . . Belonging to Him then and of Him is His Spirit; and a clear demonstration hereof will be that He can bestow It on others too and that 'not of measure,' as the blessed Evangelist saith (S. John iii. 34). For the God of all measured to the saints the grace through the Spirit.—But our Lord Jesus Christ, putting forth the Spirit out of (ἐξ) His own fulness even as

[h] Opp. vi. 98, 99, 102, 104, 105, 106.

the Father too doth, giveth it not as by measure to those worthy to have it. When the Comforter shall come, whom I will send you from the Father, the Spirit of Truth which proceedeth from the Father, He shall testify of Me. Note therefore how the Spirit which proceedeth from God the Father, this, He says, is the own Spirit of the Truth also, and He is, I suppose, full surely the Truth. How then, if He be of a truth not God Incarnate, but man rather having the Divine Indwelling as His Energy, does He promise to send down on them that believe on Him the Spirit of God the Father as though it were His own?—If then thou knowest that to sever the Spirit from His Divine Nature will be the worst of crimes, and rightly so, His, it is plain, is the Spirit, as proceeding *through* His Ineffable Nature Itself and Consubstantial with Him, and He will not need, as something external and foreign, the power from Him, but will use Him rather as His own Spirit.— And He is not putting Himself outside of being by Nature God and having the Holy Ghost as His own. —For as the Holy Ghost proceedeth out of (ἐκ) the Father, being His Spirit by Nature, in the same manner It proceedeth *through* the Son also, being His of Nature and Consubstantial with Him. Hence even if He be glorified through the Spirit, He is conceived of, as Himself glorifying Himself through His own Spirit; and this is not anything external, even if He be seen made Man as we. For the Flesh was the Word's own; and this yourself have just confessed to us (for you said that the Manhood is His and the Holy Body taken out of (ἐκ) the holy Virgin is called His Temple). His again is His Spirit, and the Word out of (ἐκ) God the Father will never be conceived of without His own Spirit."

Again in his answer to the Eastern Bishops' objection to his eleventh chapter occur the remarkable words,

> "[i] But we must know that (as we said before) it is the own body of the Word which quickeneth all things, and because it is the body of life, it is also quickening (for through it does the Son infuse His Life into our mortal bodies and undo the might of death) but the Holy Spirit of Christ also quickens us in equal wise, for *it is the Spirit that quickeneth,* as our Saviour Himself says."

These passages are remarkable, because S. Cyril is here not speaking of the relation of the Persons of the Holy Trinity one with another, but, assuming that his readers already know that God the Holy Ghost is the Very Spirit of God the Son, he is proving that, God the Son having been made Man for us, the relation of God the Holy Ghost to Him remains unaltered thereby.

Among the Latin Fathers, both modes of speech are contained, in fact, in the earliest Christian writer, who speaks at all of the Procession of God the Holy Ghost, although elaborate argument may first be found among the Greeks. The Procession of God the Holy Ghost *from* the Son, as the Third in order of the All-Holy Trinity, (as conveyed by the formula of Baptism given to us by our Lord) occurs in Tertullian, as well as the other form, involved also in that same formula, that the Father, being the Father, is the One Origin of Being in the Coeternal Trinity. The word 'through' he uses expressly.

"[k] Let me say this in regard to the third degree.

---

[i] Apol. adv. Episc. Orient. Cap. xi. Opp. vi. 193 fin. This is also exstant in Syriac in the VIth century MS. Add. 12156. British Museum.   [k] adv. Prax. c. 4. p. 636 Rig.

[the Third in order]. For I do not suppose that the Spirit is from any other, than from the Father through the Son."

The other is contained in one of those illustrations (which commended themselves to the fathers), how, in physical objects too, things might be in a manner one, which came, in order, from one. I will set down the whole passage, because the illustrations are so foreign from our mode of thought.

"[1] The tree is not severed from the root, nor the river from the fountain, nor the ray from the sun, so neither the Word from God. So then, following these examples, I profess that I speak of Two, God and His Word, the Father and His Son. For the root and the tree are two things, but conjoined. And the fountain and the river are two kinds, but undivided. And the sun and the ray are two forms, but cohering. For every thing which cometh forth from any thing, must be second to that, from which it cometh forth; but it is not therefore separated. Where there is a second, there are two; and where is a third, there are three. For the Spirit is the Third from God and the Son, as the fruit is the third from the tree. And the stream from the river is the third from the river, and the apex from the ray is the third from the sun. But nothing is alien from that matrix, from which it derives its own properties. Thus the Trinity, flowing down from the Father, through entwined and connected degrees, in no way injures the Monarchia, and guards the stato of the dispensation, which [as he had before [m] explained it] distributes the Unity into a Trinity, ordering the Three, Father Son and Spirit; Three—of one substance, of one condition, of one power."

[1] Ib. c. 8. p. 639.   [m] Ib. c. 2.

Tertullian here clearly preserves the Monarchia, but believed that God the Holy Ghost immediately proceeded from God the Son.

S. Hilary also uses both ways of speaking; and this, not in any incidental passages, but writing on the Holy Trinity against those who denied It.

> "[n] Of the Holy Spirit I neither ought to be silent, nor is it necessary to speak; but I must not be silent as to Him, Who is to be confessed of [de] the Father and the Son His Authors. Since He is, and is given and is possessed, and is of God, let the speech of the calumniators cease. When they say, through Whom is He, or for what is He, or of what sort is He, if our answer displeases when we say [by Him] by Whom are all things, [the Son], and from Whom are all things [the Father], and that He is the Spirit of God, the Gift to the faithful, be they displeased with Apostles and Prophets, saying only that He is, and after this they will be displeased with the Father and the Son."

Before, S. Hilary had spoken of the Son as the Author of His Being,

> "[o] What marvel that they think diversely of the Holy Spirit, who devise so rashly, in creating and changing and abrogating His Giver, and so dissolve the verity of this perfect mystery, essaying to introduce diversity of substance in What hath all so common, [the Father and the Son,] denying the Father, while they take from the Son, that He is a Son; denying the Holy Spirit, while they ignore Its use and Its Author!"

And more fully, while expanding our Lord's words in S. John;

[n] de Trin. ii. 29.   [o] Ib. n. 4.

"ᵖ Nor in this do I wrong liberty of understanding, whether they should think that the Spirit, the Paraclete, is from the Father or from the Son. For the Lord left it not uncertain; for He thus speaks, using the same words, "ᵠ I have yet many things to say unto you, but ye cannot bear them now. Howbeit when He, the Spirit of truth, is come, He will guide you into all truth: for He shall not speak of Himself; but whatsoever He shall hear, that shall He speak, and He will shew you things to come. He shall glorify Me, for He shall receive of Mine, and shall shew it unto you. All things that the Father hath are Mine; therefore said I, that He shall take of Mine, and shall shew it unto you."

"*He* therefore receiveth from the Son, Who is both sent by Him and proceedeth from the Father. And I ask whether it is not the self-same thing to 'receive from the Son,' and to 'proceed from the Father.' But if it shall be believed that to 'receive from the Son' is different from 'proceeding from the Father,' certainly it will seem to be one and the self-same thing, to receive from the Son, and to receive from the Father. For the Lord Himself says, 'For He shall receive of Mine, and shall shew it unto you. All things that the Father hath are Mine: therefore said I, that He shall take of Mine, and shew it unto you.'"

"This which He shall receive (whether it be power or virtue or doctrine) the Son says, shall be 'received from Him,' and again He signifies that this self-same thing is to be received from the Father. But when He saith that 'all things, whatsoever the Father hath,' are His, and that therefore He said, that His own shall be taken, He teaches also that they are to be received of the Father: yet are received of Him, because all which the Father has are His.

ᵖ Ib. viii. 20.   ᵠ S. John xvi. 12-15.

This unity has no diversity; nor does it differ, from Whom it is received, which, being given from the Father, is referred, as given from the Son. Will unity of will be introduced here too? All which the Father has, are the Son's; and all things which are the Son's are the Father's. For He saith, '*And all Mine are Thine, and Thine are Mine.'—He saith, that He [God the Holy Ghost] should receive from Him, because all things of the Father's were His. Cut in twain, if thou canst, the unity of this nature, and infer some necessity of unlikeness, through which the Son is not in unity of nature [with the Father.] For the Spirit of truth proceedeth from the Father; but He is sent by the Son from the Father. All things which the Father hath, are the Son's, and therefore whatever He Who is to be sent shall receive, He shall receive from the Son, because all things which are the Father's, are the Son's. Nature then retaineth, in all things, its own law, and that Both are one substance, indicates that there is one Divinity in both, through Generation and Birth, since what the Spirit of truth shall receive from the Father, *that*, the Son saith, is to be given from Himself. It must not then be allowed to heretical perversity, to understand in an ungodly way, that this saying of the Son, that, because all things which the Father has are His, therefore the Spirit of truth will receive from Him, is not to be referred to the unity of Nature."

S. Hilary ends his book on the Holy Trinity with a prayer to God,

"*Preserve in me, I pray, this undefiled religion of my faith, and, until my spirit departeth, grant me [to keep] this voice of my conscience, that what I professed in the Creed of my regeneration, being

---

r S. John xvii. 10.   s de Trin. xii. 56.

baptised in the Father and the Son and the Holy Ghost I may ever retain, that I should adore Thee, our Father; Thy Son with Thee; and obtain Thy Holy Spirit [t], Who is *from Thee through Thine Only-Begotten.* For He is to me a sufficient witness to my faith, Who saith 'Father, all Mine are Thine and Thine are Mine,' our Lord Jesus Christ."

He had said just before, speaking of the eternal Being of the Spirit,

"As in that, that Thine Only-Begotten was born of Thee before endless time, apart from all ambiguity of language and understanding, there remains this alone that He was born, so that *Thy Holy Spirit is from Thee through Him*, although I perceive it not by sense, yet I hold by conscience."

S. Ambrose speaks of the Holy Spirit proceeding from the Father and the Son in the same way, in which he speaks of the Son's proceeding from the Father, that He is inseparable from Those from Whom He proceedeth. He is speaking of His mission in time; yet so as to shew, that His relation to Both is the same, and that the mission in time implies the eternal relation:

"[t] Lastly Wisdom saith, that He so proceedeth from the mouth of the Most Highest, as not to be without the Father, but with the Father, because 'The Word was *with* God:' and not only *with* the Father, but *in* the Father, For He saith, "[u] I am in the Father, and the Father is in Me." But neither, when He goeth forth from the Father, doth He remove from place, or is separated, as a body from a body: nor when He is in the Father, is He included as a body in a body; the Holy Spirit, when He proceedeth from the Father and the Son, is not separated

[t] de Sp. S. i. 11. n. 120. Ben.   [u] S. John xiv. 11.

from the Father, is not separated from the Son. For how can He be separated from the Father Who is the Spirit of His Mouth? Which both implies eternity and expresses the Unity of Divinity."

And again,

"ᵛBoth the Son proceedeth from the Father and the Spirit proceedeth from Himself. There is then nothing doubtful about the Unity of Divinity."

Elsewhere he argues that goodness may be predicated of the Son, because it is predicated of the Spirit Who receives of Them,

"ʷIf it moveth any one, that 'No one is good, save One God,' let that too move him, that no one is good, save God. But if the Son is not excepted from being God, neither is Christ excepted from the good. For since in God, the Son is Another in Person, One in power (for there is One God, from Whom are all things, and One Lord, through Whom are all things: but God and Lord are not two Gods, but One God, since 'the Lord thy God is One Lord,') so since both Persons are in Majesty One God, One God is in Both. How is He not good, Who is born of One Good?—How is He not good, since *the substance of goodness*, taken from the Father, degenerated not in the Son, which did not degenerate in the Spirit? And therefore 'Thy good Spirit shall lead me in the right way!' But if the Spirit is good, Who received from the Son, good also is He Who gave;"

where that which is given must be His eternal Being.

S. Augustine often teaches us that the temporal mission involves the Eternal Procession, upon which it is founded:

"ˣAs the Father begat, the Son was Begotten, so

ᵛ in Ps. 16. n. 9.   ʷ in S. Lucam L. 8. n. 66. Opp. i. 1487 Ben.
ˣ de Trin. L. xiv. n. 29. Opp. viii. p. 827.

the Father sent, the Son was sent. But as He Who begat and He Who was Begotten, so He Who sent and He Who was sent are one Substance, because the Father and the Son are one Substance. So the Holy Spirit also is one Substance with Them, because these Three are one Substance. For as, to the Son, to be born is to be from [a] the Father, so to be sent, is to be known that He is from [a] Him. And as, to the Spirit, to be the Gift of God is to proceed from [a] the Father, so to be sent, is to be known that He proceedeth from [a] Him. Nor can we say that the Holy Spirit doth not proceed also from [a] the Son; for not in vain is He, the same Spirit, said to be the Spirit both of the Father and the Son. Nor do I see what else He willed to signify, when, breathing on the face of the disciples, He said, 'Receive the Holy Spirit.' For neither was that bodily breath, proceeding from the body with sense of bodily touch, the Substance of the Holy Spirit, but a demonstration, through a fitting significance, that the Holy Spirit proceeded, not only from [a] the Father, but from [a] the Son also. For who were so exceeding mad as to say, that it was one Spirit, Whom He gave by breathing on them, and another whom He sent after His Resurrection? For One is the Spirit of God, the Spirit of the Father and the Son, the Holy Spirit, Who worketh all things in all.—His saying then 'Whom I will send unto you from the Father' shews that He is the Spirit both of the Father and the Son. Since moreover, when He had said 'Whom the Father will send,' He added 'in My Name,' He did not yet say 'Whom the Father will send from Me,' as He said, 'Whom I will send unto you from the Father,' this was to shew that the Father is the Beginning [or Principle] of the whole Divinity, or (if it is best so to speak) Deity. He then, Who proceedeth from the Father and the Son, is referred to Him, from Whom the Son is born."

As S. Augustine asserts the Monarchia distinctly in regard to the Procession of the Holy Spirit, that "the Father is the Beginning, or Principium of the whole Trinity," so he subsequently states that the Holy Ghost proceeds "principially from the Father:"

> "[y] Not in vain in this Trinity is none called the Word of God save the Son, nor the Gift of God save the Spirit, nor He from Whom the Word is Begotten, and from Whom principially the Holy Spirit proceedeth, save God the Father. I therefore added 'principially,' because the Holy Spirit is found to proceed from the Son also. But this also the Father gave Him, not to Him already existing and not as yet having it, but, whatever He gave to the Only-Begotten Word, He gave by Begetting. He then so begat Him, that from [de] Him also that common Gift should proceed, and the Holy Spirit be the Spirit of Both."

Further on, he assigns this as the ground, why the word "Begotten" is used of God the Son; "proceeding," of God the Holy Ghost,

> "He who can understand the Generation of the Son from the Father without time may understand the Procession of the Holy Spirit from Both without time. And he who, in that which the Son saith, 'As the Father hath life in Himself, so He hath given to the Son to have life in Himself,' can understand that the Father gave life to the Son, not as existing already without life, but that He so without time begat Him, that the life, which the Father gave by begetting is coeternal with the life of the Father Who gave it, he would understand that as the Father

[y] de Trin. xv. n. 29. p. 988.

hath in Himself, that the Holy Spirit should proceed of Him, so He gave to the Son, that the same Holy Spirit should proceed from Him, and both without time; and that this Holy Spirit so proceedeth from the Father, that it should be understood, that the Son hath from the Father, that He proceedeth also from Him. For if whatever the Son hath, He hath from the Father, then He hath this, that the Holy Spirit proceedeth from Him also: but no before or after must be thought of therein, since then time was not. How then would it not be most absurd to call Him the Son of Both, since, as Generation from the Father without any mutability of Nature bestoweth Essence upon the Son without beginning of time, so, without any mutability of Nature, Procession from Both bestoweth Essence on the Holy Spirit without any beginning of time? For therefore, whereas we do not call the Holy Spirit Begotten, we do not yet venture to call Him Unbegotten, lest, under this word, any one should suspect that there are two Fathers in that Trinity, or two Who have not their Being from another. For the Father Alone is not from Another, therefore He Alone is called Unbegotten, not indeed in the Scriptures, but in the common use of those who discuss thereon, and in so high a matter utter such language as they are able. But the Son is Born of the Father, and the Holy Spirit proceedeth principially from the Father, and by His gift, without any interval of time, in common from Both. But He would be called the Son of the Father and of the Son, if, (which were abhorrent from all sane understanding,) Both had Begotten Him. The Spirit then was not Begotten by Both, but proceedeth from Each of the Twain."

"But since in that Co-Eternal, and Equal, and Incorporeal, and Ineffably Unchangeable, and Inseparable Trinity, it is most difficult to distinguish

Generation from Procession, let that suffice for those who cannot reach out further, which on this subject I have spoken in a Sermon to the ears of the Christian people, and have since written down. Having taught by testimonies of Holy Scripture, that the Holy Spirit proceedeth from Both, I said, [z] How then, if the Holy Spirit proceedeth from the Father and the Son, doth the Son say, He proceedeth from the Father? Why, thinkest thou, save that, as He is wont to refer to Him, what belongs to Himself, from Whom He Himself is? Whence also He saith, 'My doctrine is not Mine, but His Who sent Me.' If then, in this place, the doctrine is understood to be His, which yet He said is not His, but the Father's, how much more in that other place is the Holy Spirit to be understood to proceed from Himself, when He saith, He proceedeth from the Father, yet not so as to say, 'He proceedeth not from Me!' For from Whom the Son hath, that He is God, (for He is God from God,) from Him He hath accordingly, that the Holy Spirit should proceed from Him. And thereby the Spirit hath from the Father Himself this, that He should proceed from the Son, as He proceedeth from the Father. Hence also that may be understood, as far as can be understood by such as we are, why the Holy Spirit is not said to be born, but rather to proceed. For if He too were called Son, He would be called the Son of Both, which would be most absurd. For no son is of two, save of father and mother. But God forbid that we should imagine anything of this sort as to God the Father and God the Son. For not even among men doth a son proceed at once from father and mother. But the Holy Spirit doth not proceed from the Father into the Son, and proceed from the Son to

---

[z] This sermon is the 99th homily on S. John n. 8. 9, pp. 921-923. Oxf. Tr.

sanctify the creature, but proceeds from Both together, although the Father gave this to the Son, that as the Spirit proceeds from Himself, so He should proceed from Him. For neither can we say that the Spirit is not Life, since the Father is Life, the Son is Life, and thereby, as the Father, having Life in Himself, gave to the Son also to have Life in Himself, so also He gave Him, that Life should proceed from Him, even as He proceedeth from Himself." "This," S. Augustine adds, " I have transferred from that sermon into this book, but speaking to believers not to unbelievers."

He meets herein an objection current among the Arians. Maximinus asked him, "If the Son is of the substance of the Father, and the Holy Spirit is of the substance of the Father, why is One, Son, and the Other, not Son?" He says,

"[a] I answer, whether thou takest it in or no, the Son is from the Father, the Holy Spirit is from the Father; but the One, Begotten; the Other, Proceeding. Therefore the One is the Son of the Father, of Whom He is Begotten, the Other is the Spirit of Both, because He proceedeth from Both. But therefore, when the Son spake of Him, He said, He proceedeth from the Father, because the Father is the Author of His Procession, Who begat such a Son, and, by begetting, bestowed upon Him, that the Holy Spirit should proceed from Him. For unless He proceeded from Himself also, He would not say to His disciples, 'Receive the Holy Spirit,' and give Him by breathing on them, so as to signify that He proceeded from Himself, and shew this openly by breathing, what secretly He gave by inspiring. Since then, if He were born, He would be born not only from the Father, nor only from the

[a] cont. Maximin. Ar. ii. 14.

Son, but from Both, He would be called the Son of Both; and because He is nowise the Son of Both, He ought not to be born of Both. He is then the Spirit of Both by proceeding from Both [b]."

These Latin fathers [c], S. Hilary, S. Ambrose and S. Augustine have been quoted as authorities on other matters of doctrine at General Councils, and so have been formally acknowledged as authorities in the Church by the Greeks also. At the Council of Ephesus [d], S. Cyril quoted S. Ambrose as well as S. Cyprian: at the end of the tome of S. Leo, read at the Council of Chalcedon [e], are quoted S. Hilary Bishop and Confessor, S. Augustine, Bishop of Hippo, with S. Gregory of Nazianzus, and S. Chrysostom and S. Cyril; in the 5th General Council [f], S. Augustine was quoted; in the 6th [g], S. Augustine and S. Ambrose are quoted, as holy and select fathers, together with S. Athanasius and S. Chrysostom: and in a later session S. Ambrose, S. Augustine, and S. Leo. S. Leo was the centre of the Fourth General Council, as S. Cyril was of the Third. The representatives of the East then at Bonn, when they "acknowledged the representation of the doctrine of the Holy Ghost, as it is set forth by the fathers of the undivided Church," only did what their forefathers had done in the General Councils. We have only to pray God, for His Son's sake, to

[b] See also serm. cont. Arian. c. 23. Opp. viii. 639, 640. Pet. 1. c.
[c] In Ruffinus (de symbolo n. 35. p. 99 Ben.) whom Bellarmine quoted (de Christo ii. 4. Contr. i. 421) the reading seems uncertain.   [d] Act. i. Conc. iii. 1057 Col.
[e] Act. ii. Conc. iv. 1227-1238.   [f] Act. v. Conc. vi. 95, 96 Col.
[g] Act. viii. Conc. vii. 789. Act. x. 815, sqq.

give them grace to act according to their pledge, and in the spirit of their great fathers.

I have already set down in succession 15 other Latin fathers [h] earlier than the Third Council of Toledo, which received the *Filioque,* in their own verbal agreement and others prior to the VIth General Council. Probably, except perhaps S. Leo, they were not mentioned at the Council of Florence. For few of the Greeks probably understood Latin. Scholarius, in his proposed formula of agreement, did not even mention the Latin fathers [i]. The Council however, alluded to them in its definition [k], and the Patriarch who had been averse to the Latin formula, gave his vote in writing thus,

> "[l] Since we have heard the sayings of the holy Eastern and Western fathers, some saying, that the Holy Spirit proceedeth from the Father and the Son, others, that He is from the Father through the Son, (although the 'through the Son' is the same as 'from the Son,' and 'from the Son' is the same as 'through the Son,') yet we, leaving the ' from the Son,' say that the Holy Spirit proceedeth from the Father through the Son eternally and essentially as from origin and cause, the 'through' designating 'cause' in the Procession of the Holy Spirit."

To all this the Bishops assented, except five; among them, Mark of Ephesus. Syropulus says that the Patriarch had told him why he had subscribed to the union. These grounds were his dying bequest to the Greek Church. For the Patriarch was now beyond human hopes or fears, having nothing

[h] See ab. pp. 53-61.   [i] Ib. p. 102.   [k] Ib. p. 104.
[l] Syropulus sect. 9. c. 9. Le Qu. xxviii.

before him but the eternity, at whose opening doors he was lying. The grounds were,

> "that the writings of the Western fathers were genuine; that he had read Athanasius, affirming the same; also Cyril in various places; Epiphanius too whose words were so express, that Joseph [m], Monk and Doctor, once owned candidly, that he had what to answer to passages of other fathers, but to the Saint himself, nothing."

The language and thoughts of S. Augustine agreeing, as he does, with him who is known as Dionysius the Areopagite, "[n]the Father is Sole Fountain of the Supersubstantial Deity," or with their own S. Basil, that the Son is "[o]immediately" ($ἀμέσως$ or $προσέχως$) from the Father, the holy Spirit "[p]intermediately" ($ἐμμέσως$); or that the Father is the principal ([p]$προκαταρκτικὴ$) Cause might, I hope, especially be a meeting-point of both. I would venture in this sense to suggest an additional proposition to those accepted last year at Bonn,

> "The Holy Ghost proceedeth from the Father and the Son together as being essentially One but *principially* from the Father."

This agreement of the Greek and Latin fathers is so complete, that it needs no further witness. Yet it is interesting to see the agreement of the farthest East. We have heard a Syrian Bishop confessing the Procession of the Holy Ghost from the

---

[m] Bp. of Methone probably, A.D. 1440, who wrote Responsio ad libellum Marci Ephesii, inserted in App. to Council of Florence Conc. xviii. p. 690.

[n] T. i. 2. 4. 7. ap. Pet. vii. 17. 8. [o] Petav. de Trin. vii. 11.

[p] S. Basil de Sp. S. c. 16.

Father and the Son q. The Council of Seleucia and Ctesiphon A. D. 410 confesses that Procession in exactly the same way, as S. Epiphanius, who died A.D. 402, being 115 years old. For as S. Epiphanius, three times, says of God the Holy Ghost, Who "ʳ is of the Father and the Son," not using the word "proceeding," so also the Council of Seleucia ˢ. Renaudot, a competent judge, says ᵗ, " of the antiquity and authority of that Creed there ought to be no doubt." S. Maruthas, who, with his brother Isaac, presided over that Council, and who is related to have brought thither the Canons of Nice, has long been known to us as a Bishop of Mesopotamia ᵘ, who, on two occasions ᵛ, was sent on an embassy by the Greek Emperor to Isdegerd king of Persia. Isdegerd was much impressed with his piety, had him

  q See ab. p. 123.   r See ab. pp. 119-121.
 s I am indebted for my first knowledge of this Council to the kindness of the Abbé Martin of Paris, who, on occasion of my letter in the Times, wrote me a letter which he has since published under the title, " La double Procession du Saint Esprit et la conference de Bonn." He writes on the Council and its genuineness p. 18. sqq. The Creed was published by Card. Pitra from the MS. in the Ambrosian library, (placed there by Card. Borromeo) in his Juris Eccl. Græcorum hist. et monum. T. i. p. xliii-xlvii.; the entire Council by Lamy Concilium Seleuciæ et Ctesiphonti habitum A. 410, &c. to which I am indebted for the proofs of its genuineness, which I have simply verified. I am also indebted to the Abbé Martin for directing my attention to Renaudot and Assemani.
 t " The 2nd Canon contains an exposition of faith, in which, since there is no trace of Nestorian or Jacobite doctrine, it agrees plainly with the right faith, which Maruthas professed, and with his age, nor ought there to be any doubt as to its antiquity and authority." Liturgg. Orient. ii. 272, 273.
  u Socr. vi. 15.   v Id. vii. 8.

in much honour, having by his prayer been cured of a chronic suffering, which the Magi had not been able to cure. Socrates, a younger contemporary, tells us how he detected frauds of the Magi, stood in increased favour with Isdegerd, whom he almost converted, and who allowed him to build Churches, where he willed. Maruthas, the embassy, on which he was sent to Isdegerd, and the Council which he held, are mentioned by a learned and orthodox Syrian Bishop, known as " the Persian preacher [w]," who lived a century later, A.D. 510, Simeon Bishop of Beth-Arsham. In his Epistle on Barsumas Bishop of Nisibis and the Nestorian heresy, he says,

> "[x] They separated themselves from the faith—which they confirmed and ratified in the time of Maruthas the Bishop, (who was sent on an embassy from Cæsar king of the Romans to Isdegerd king of kings in the 11th year of his reign,) with 40 Bishops of the kingdom of Persia."

This corresponds with the title of the Canons of the Synod.

> "[y] Some canons and rules, which were enacted by the Synod of Persian Bishops, in Seleucia and Ctesiphon, cities of the dominion of the kingdom of the Persians, when Maruthas Bishop of Maiphercat was sent on an embassy to king Isdegerd, in the 11th year of that Isdegerd, son of king Sapor. There were gathered 40 Bishops in Seleucia and Ctesiphon; their heads were Isaac, Catholicus and Archbishop of the same Seleucia and Ctesiphon, and Maruthas, his brother. And they sat in the great Church of

---

[w] Or " disputer," [doroosho]. He converted some magi, and wrote against Nestorians. Assem. B. O. i. c. 29 pp. 341. sqq.

[x] Ib. p. 355.

[y] Conc. Seleuc. et Ctesiphon. A. 410. Canones, p. 22.

Seleucia and Ctesiphon in the month Shebot (Feb⁷.) on the 3rd day of the week. And they read the epistle which was sent them from the West [viz. of Persia], from the Bishops who were gathered in the land of the Romans [viz. Constantinople, as 'new Rome'], and these canons were read which were enacted in the West. They enacted the canons below."

Isdegerd died A.D. 420 ᶻ; his 11th year then was in A.D. 410.

"ᵃ Since then the Synod of Seleucia preceded the date of the heresies of Nestorius and Eutyches, its canons are received by the Jacobites and Nestorians with the same reverence as by the Catholics."

Of the Nestorians, Elias of Damascus (ixth cent.) mentions the Synod, Canons and Creed, in detail,

"ᵇ He who brought the laws and canons, which the Bishops of Room (Greece) from time to time sent to the East, and translated the laws of the 318 Bishops assembled at Nice, from Greek to Syriac, was Maruthas Bishop of Amida and Miapharekin, when he came to Isdegerd king of Persia with the letter from the king of Room; and the Catholicus in the East at that time was Isaac; and when he and Maruthas met at Modain, they asked leave of the

---

ᶻ The martyrdom of "James the mangled" is dated in the 2nd. year of his son Vararan, in the 732nd year of the Seleucidæ. Assem. Acta Mart. i. 241. But Isdegerd reigned 21 years, according to Barhebræus and others quoted by Lamy Conc. Seleuc. et Ctesiph. col. 10.   ᵃ Lamy Ib. col. 12, 13.

ᵇ In Assem. Bibl. Or. iii. 1. p. 367. Abulpharaj Benattib, a Nestorian monk xi cent., in his index of constitutions statutes and canons of Eastern and Western Councils, mentioned 26 canons of Isaac, Catholicus or Primate of Seleucia and Ctesiphon in the Council of Seleucia A.D. 410 under the same Isaac and Maruthas Bishop of Tekrit. Assem. Catal. Codd. Orient. Biblioth. Med. p. 94.

king to assemble the Bishops of the East, that they might look into those laws, and consider about keeping them. He gave them leave. 40 Metropolitans and Bishops assembled to Isaac and Maruthas, (this was in the 11th year of Isdegerd). So Maruthas read them the aforesaid laws and the Creed which the 318 Bishops agreed upon. So they received this and approved of it, and anathematised whoever contradicted it. And they wrote a book, and inserted in it the faith, and the laws, chapter by chapter, and matter by matter, and they inserted their names, man by man, according to his degree, Metropolitans and Bishops, and the name of the see over which he presided, and they sealed it with their seals."

Ebedjesu also in his collection of Canons [c] frequently inserts Canons of this Council.

Of the Jacobites, Bar-hebræus, a writer so well known among us also as a historian, gives the following account of the Synod of A.D. 410.

"[d]And Maruthas of Maipherkat was sent a second time on an embassy to Isdegerd in his 11th year, and he made known to Isaac the Catholicus concerning the cause of the Synod. And Isaac collected 40 Bishops of his. These agreed to the deposition of Macedonius. And this Maruthas de-

[c] "Published by A. Mai Scriptt. Vett. nova Coll. T. x." "In Ebedjesu's tract. viii. c. 17. he quotes verbatim can. 3 and 27 'from the *synod of Isaac*,' who presided over it: in tract. vi. c. 6, can. 16 he quotes the whole of can. 4; tract. viii. c. 1 and 9 he transcribes nearly verbatim can. 3; and tract. ix. c. 5, canon 8. He mentions also acts of the synod of Isaac, Ib. viii. 15." Lamy Ib. col. 13.

[d] From the part of his Chronicle, still unpublished. Lamy published the Syriac, (furnished him from the MS. of the British Museum Rich. 7198 by I. B. Abbeloos) l. c. col. 3.

fined for them admirable canons, and taught the Easterns the beauty of discipline. And Isaac ministered for 11 years and departed and was buried in Seleucia."

His collection of Canons also has been published [e]. It also embodies Canons of the Council of Seleucia under the name "of the Persians [f]," because the Council consisted of Persian Bishops. But "[g] the Monophysites and Nestorians never borrow from one another; the common authorities, to which they refer, are always prior to the great heresies of the 5th. century."

"[g] The MS. from which the Creed has been printed, is Monophysite and contains no piece taken from the Persian Church, later than the Council of Ephesus."

The Abbé Martin, who has recently examined the MS. from which the Council has been published, assures us, that it contains nothing later than the 7th century [h]. The Paris MS. he and the learned curator of the Syrian MSS. of the Paris library, assign to the 8th or 9th century (at latest, then, not later than Photius A.D. 858 and the origin of the schism [i].) Nor is there the possibility of interpola-

[e] Nomocanon in Latin by A. Mai Vett. Scriptt. nova coll. T. x.
[f] In c. 1, s. 4, he quotes Canon 17 : c. v. s. 5, he quotes canon 18, and refers to 20, 21 : cap. vi. s. 2, he quotes canon 10: cap. vii. s. 6, he quotes canon 19.
[g] l'Abbé Martin, La double Procession p. 19.   [h] Ib. p. 22.
[i] Card. Dom. Pitra says "I find in my papers, that the San German MS. was written at Nitriæ in 1166 of the Greek era : =A.D. 795, from a note at the end," so that it is a dated MS. Jur. Eccl. Græc. T. i. p. xlv. Renaudot says of the Florentine MS., "The Florentine MS. is, at least, more than 700 years [in 1716] and the confession itself is more ancient than the schism of the Nestorians and Jacobites." Renaudot ii. 274.

tion. The Syriac words stand at the beginning of the line, and are in the same hand as the rest of the MS [k]. In the same MS. also the Creed of Constantinople occurs, without the addition [k]. This shews that the transcriber did not transcribe, under any bias.

I have given the evidence in the more detail, because two writers of repute, who had seen only a Latin translation of the Council, have spoken in an off-hand way about it. Muratori merely throws out a sarcasm, that perhaps Card. Borromeo had been imposed upon. He acknowledges the value of the Council, were it, as it is, genuine. He says,

> "[1] I subjoin, not a figment, but a doubtful monument, a Syriac Synod, hitherto, I trow, seen by no one, which Frederic Card. Borromeo, Archbishop of Milan, had translated from Syriac, and deposited in the Ambrosian library, which he formed, from which I took it. And would that, as that Synod primâ facie has the look of a venerable antiquity, so it might be pronounced a genuine and most ancient product! But this I cannot say, fearing lest some Syrian should have imposed upon the most learned Cardinal, hoping for gain from such merchandise."

Muratori owned that the translation, which he read and published, had the appearance of antiquity, and, for fear of being deceived, was deceived.

It is the more to be regretted that Bishop Hefele should have rejected the Council [m], without informing himself on the subject. He argues against it,

[k] l' Abbé Martin ib. p. 22.
[l] Antiq. Ital. medii ævi, iii. 976.
[m] Hefele, History of the Councils ii. 445. I quote from the careful translation, having only the 1st. edit. of the original.

1) because a later Syriac author supposed Arcadius to have sent the embassy : but the fact of the embassy is certain from a contemporary Greek writer[n], and the mistake of a later Syriac writer about the name of a Greek Emperor is of no moment. The earlier Syriac writers do not name the Emperor. 2) because "some of its canons are founded on the Nicene," which the Council of Seleucia professedly was. 3) because it states the double Procession; but so did the contemporary S. Epiphanius in the self-same way [o].

Syriac scholars could not and have not doubted about the Council or its Creed; and there have now been several [p].

The Preface to the Synod says,

"After they [the 40 Bishops under Isaac and Maruthas] had read the letter, which was sent them from the West, from the Bishops who were gathered in the land of the Romans, and there were written in it these Canons, which were enacted in the West, they themselves enacted these Canons which are written below."

The second Canon is entitled;

"The faith which was laid down by the Bishops of Persia. 'We believe in One God the Father, Who holdeth all things; Him, Who by His Son made heaven and earth, and by Him were framed the worlds above and below; by Him He made the resurrection and joy to the whole creation; And in His only Son Who was begotten of Him, that is,

[n] Socrates, ab. p. 150.   [o] See ab. pp. 119-121.
[p] Renaudot; Card. Dom. Pitra; a Syriac scholar, who "examined all the books at Milan which could throw light upon it, and wrote a thick volume with preface and notice" (Pitra Juris eccl. T. i. Pref. p. xliv.); Lamy; Abbé Martin; Zotenberg.

of the Essence of His Father, God of God, Light of Light, Very God of Very God, Begotten, not made: Who is the Son of the Substance of [consubstantial with [q]] His Father; Who for us men who were created by His Hands, and for our salvation, came down and was clothed with a body and was made Man; and suffered and rose on the third day, and ascended into heaven and sat on the Right Hand of the Father, and cometh to judge the quick and dead. And we confess the living Holy Spirit, the living Paraclete, Who is from the Father and the Son, in One Trinity, in One Essence, in One Will, in harmony with the faith of the 318 Bishops, which was in the city of Nice. And it is our confession, and our faith, which we have received from our holy fathers." "The definition which was made by the holy Synod." —

I have given the whole Creed, as not identical with any other Creed, although containing portions of the Nicene. It has no marked addition from the Creed of Constantinople. It may have been, on some grounds connected with Persia for which it was framed, that the resurrection was placed thus early in the Creed. The Creed is not said to be the Creed of Nice, but in harmony with it, as at the end of the Canons they are called,

"[r] The Canons, laid down by the Synod of Persian Bishops, *as* from the force of the Canons of the great Synod of Nice."

The Double Procession must have been held by the orthodox Syrians, since both Nestorians and Eutychians took it with them from the Church,

[q] As in the Chaldæan Missal, p. 279. Lamy, p. 30.
[r] Lamy p. 36.

although they gradually lost it, as heretics. But heretics, although they gradually lose faith, which they took with them from the Church, never gain any which they had not, when they left it.

The Nestorians "in their Office which they call the Announcing, i.e. the 4th Lord's day before the Nativity of the Lord, have at Matins [s],

> "God is One, Who is altogether Incomprehensible and is in Three Persons, Who have no beginning: the Eternal Father, Who hath no Father; and the Son from Him, Who hath no Son; and the Holy Spirit Who proceedeth from Them; a Nature, which containeth all things; to Him be praise in the temple of our humanity."

They had not the Confession in their Creed. For Elias, their Patriarch, writing to Paul V. on the differences between the Roman Church and the Nestorians, says [t],

> "The Lord Pope with all the fathers of the great Roman Church say, that the Holy Spirit proceedeth from the Father and the Son: but we confess that the Spirit proceedeth from the Father."

Yet Adam, an Archimandrite, while yet a Nestorian, inferred, in manner of the great fathers, that the Procession from the Father implied the Procession from the Son also.

> "[u] But of the Holy Spirit, 'Who proceedeth from the Father,' as the Easterns confess, and the fathers of the Church of great Rome, who confess that 'He proceedeth from the Father and the Son,' both acknowledge the truth, and one true testimony sufficeth

---

[s] in Assem. diss. de Syr. Nest. Bibl. Or. iii. 2. ccxxxv.
[t] in Strozzi, de dogm. Chaldæor. p. 17. in Ass. l. c. p. ccxxxiv.
[u] in Strozzi l. c. p. 32 quoted Ib.

for true believers; viz. that Word which was uttered by the most beloved Jesus, "I and My Father are One Substance," and He Himself said, they are One, and did not say 'We are like.' But they are One Substance, and not two. But if they are One, and not two, what difference is there between what we confess, viz. that 'the Holy Spirit proceedeth from the Father,' and that, that He 'proceedeth from the Father and the Son?' So, They are One Substance, and not two, and there is no division between Them. He said also, 'I am in My Father, and My Father in Me,' and, 'Whoso seeth Me, seeth Him Who sent Me.' But of the Holy Spirit He said, 'He shall receive of Mine, and shall shew it unto you;' 'All which the Father hath, is Mine;' and if thus there is no division between the Incomprehensible Persons of the Hidden Deity, without any before or after, any lesser or greater, any having or not having, in all things, who shall put any difference between that saying, 'The Spirit proceedeth from the Father,' and that, 'The Spirit proceedeth from the Father and the Son?' But the Easterns say that He 'proceedeth from the Father,' because they know that the Father possesseth nothing which the Son hath not, nor the Son, which the Father hath not. As they have learned from the Living Son, Who said to the Father, 'All that I have is Thine, and what Thou hast, is Mine,' and the fathers of the great Church wished to shew that the Son is not inferior to the Father in anything, not in Essence, not in Sonship, not in Power, not in Creation, since He is 'the Brightness of His Glory, and the Image of His Essence, and upholdeth all things by the Word of His Power,' Very God of Very God, of One Substance with His Father, by Whom all things were made, they say therefore that the health-giving Spirit proceedeth from the Father and the Son; and this profession without doubt is true."

"ᵛ Jaballaha, Patriarch of the Chaldæans, in his Epistle to Benedict XI., calleth the Holy Spirit, 'the Spirit of the Father and the Son.'

> "Wherefore for the guidance of the faithful, we say, the Father is He, Who generateth, or speaketh, that the Son is the Generated, or the Word, and that the Holy Spirit is the Spirit or Life both of the Word, and of the speaker."

The Jacobite liturgy, known under the name of S. Xystus, has the prayer,

> "ʷ Have mercy upon me, O Lord, and Thy whole flock and inheritance, and accept and sanctify these oblations by the descent of Thy Holy Spirit, Who from eternity proceeds from Thee and receives from Thy Son substantially."

Upon which Renaudot says,

> "ˣThese words, which designate not unclearly the Procession of the Holy Spirit from the Father and the Son, might create a suspicion of interpolation, did not the like Theology occur in other liturgies, whose integrity is certain. In the Liturgy of Ignatius, Patriarch of Antioch, and in some others the same occurs, with this only difference, that elsewhere it is, 'and receives from the Son what are of the Substance,' or 'what are Essential;' which has the same meaning in other words. Hence it appears that the Easterns interpret our Lord's words as to the Holy Spirit, 'He shall take of Mine,' not of the gifts to be conferred on the faithful, but of the Procession through the Son. And indeed when Peter Bishop of Melicha, Paul of Sidon, Abulbircat, Ibnassal and others enumerate the errors of the Franks, they do not blame the doctrine, but the addition of the Filioque to the Creed."

ᵛ in Raynald A. 1304. p. 25. Assem. l. c.
ʷ Renaudot Liturgg. Orient. ii. p. 136.   ˣ Ib. p. 144.

In the Liturgy, which they have called the Liturgy of S. Clement of Rome [y], the Invocation of the Holy Spirit is,

> "[z] Send to us from the habitation of Thine everlasting kingdom, and from the region of Thy lofty Presence, Thy Holy Spirit, consubstantial with Thee and equal in operation, Who proceedeth from Thee, without beginning, through Thine only-Begotten Son, and Who at all times is given to those who are acceptable to Thee, and perfects and consummates those who see and understand Thee."

Renaudot remarks [a],

> "The words, 'Who proceedeth from Thee without beginning through Thine Only-begotten Son,' do not occur in other liturgies, nor in prayers of another kind. In the Syriac of S. James and in some others, there occur, 'Who proceedeth from Thee and Who receiveth from Thy Son what appertain to the essence or $\tau\grave{\alpha}$ $o\mathring{v}\sigma\iota\acute{\omega}\delta\eta$,' which so express the doctrine of the Procession of the Holy Spirit, that they are rejected by the schismatic Greeks. This testimony is not to be despised, whatever be the character of that liturgy. For it is most certain, that it has not been interpolated. And so it is clear that the belief in the Procession of the Holy Spirit 'from the Father and the Son,' or 'through the Son,' (which the Greeks acknowledge to be the same) had not its birth among the Latins, since, in the middle of Syria, witnesses thereof are

---

[y] Renaudot says, "no reason can be given why the Jacobites attributed it to Clement, except that they wished to gain estimation for their Office by the name of an Apostolic man, whose name they sometimes mention in their diptychs, and from whom they quote in their Collectanea in support of their opinion.

[z] Renaudot p. 191. He says that "the version is made from a good MS. (bonæ notæ), Colbert. 3921. Ib. p. 200. [a] Ib.

found, among those alien from the Roman communion."

In the liturgy which they have ascribed to S. Maruthas there occur the words,

"[b] Who proceedeth from Thee and receiveth from the Son."

That of Dionysius Barsalibi has

"[c] The Holy Spirit, Who proceedeth from the Father, and receiveth from the Son."

The liturgy, ascribed to S. Matthew the shepherd, has,

"[d] By the mercies, which by nature belong to Thee, O Lord, and the readiness to forgive, from which Thou art called, send the Paraclete, the Spirit of Truth, Who everlastingly proceedeth from Thee, and receiveth from the Son what pertaineth to the Substance."

In that of Ignatius Patriarch of Antioch, there is,

"[e] We pray Thee, by the abundance of Thy substantial and natural mercy, send that Thy directing Holy Spirit, Who proceedeth from Thee and receives from Thy Son essentially and from eternity."

in which the "receiving from the Son" is spoken of as being "essential and from eternity" as well as the proceeding from the Father.

Of individual Monophysites, Xenaias of Mabug A.D. 485, (as Assemani points out) admitted it in principle, since he says,

"[f] The Father differs from The Son *in this only*, that He begat and was not begotten; and again the

[b] Renaudot ii. 274. [c] Ib. p. 450. [d] Ib. p. 349.
[e] Ib. p. 533. [f] Assem. B. O. ii. 21.

> Son from the Father, that He was begotten and did not beget; so again the Holy Spirit also [differs] from the Father and the Son, that He was always Holy Spirit and not Father and not Son."

For this leaves the relation of Both Father and Son to the Holy Spirit, the same; for since the Son had all which the Father had, except being the Father, then He has also, from the Father and with the Father, the Spiration of the Holy Spirit. In this case the words of Xenaias,

> "[g] For not as the Son is from the Father, in like way also is the Spirit from the Son, but Both are from the Father. The Father is Only Essence; and the Son, Son of the Essence; and the Spirit from the Essence,"

would be to be understood (which is all that it apparently means) of the *original* source of Being.

Dionysius iii, the 83rd of their Patriarchs A.D. 933-953, has

> "[h] We believe and confess One God, Holy Trinity. The existence of the Father is from none, since He exists unbegotten; and the Son is the Begotten from eternity, and the Holy Spirit issueth forth from the Father and the Son."

Where the remark of an annotator that

> The word 'promanation' which he used, differs from "Procession," "because in what follows he uses Procession, of the Father *primarily*,"

would, if true, prove nothing, since all know that the Father is the primary Source of the Godhead, and, further, (as Assemani shews) the two words are used together, as equivalent.

[g] Assem. B. O. ii. 20.   [h] Ib. ii. 132.

Individually however the Monophysites seem mostly to have abandoned the faith expressed in their liturgies.

Bar-hebræus, however, seems to have in his mind other Jacobites who held it, when he asks,

"[i] Since Procession is the property of the Spirit, why is it added in theologies, that He receiveth from the Son? We answer, that it is on account of the manifestation to the creation, that it is most proper to say, that the Spirit receiveth from the Son.—And as for what is said by some, that He receiveth might, or power, or will, or any thing of that sort, this is a wrong opinion."

The Armenians declared their belief most clearly in the Council of Shiragvan [k], A.D. 862, held in consequence of an Epistle of Photius. This Council condemned the heresies of Nestorius, Eutyches, the Manichees and Theopaschites [l], acknowledged in an indirect way the Council of Chalcedon by condemning Eutyches: while condemning [m] those, who knowing the decision of the Council of Chalcedon and others following it to be false, did, out of human respect, not condemn them, and those who knowing the *holy* Council of Chalcedon and the three following Councils viz. the 5th, 6th, and 7th to be true and consentient with the doctrines of the Apostles and Prophets and the three preceding Councils, condemned them. While acknowledging the Council of Chalcedon thus timidly, for fear of divisions among themselves, it said plainly in its first Canon,

[i] Ass. B. O. ii. 287.

[k] Conc. x. 223 sqq. Col. from Galani Conc. Eccl. Armenæ cum Rom. T. i. Part. 2. who published it in Armenian with a Latin translation. [l] Can. 8. [m] Can. 13, 14. See Galanus l.c.

"If any one confess not the One Nature and Three Persons of the All-holy and life-giving Trinity, i.e. the Father from no Beginning, The Son from the Father, and the Holy Spirit from the same (i.e. the Father and the Son) in Essence[n], and Co-equal to Them, let him be anathema."

The old faith of the Armenian Churches was attested solemnly in the name of them all at the Council[o] of "all the Armenians" held A.D. 1342 by "[p] the Catholicon of all the Armenians, with the counsel of all the Bishops, masters, Abbots of monasteries, and some other ecclesiastics qualified thereto," at which were present 6 Archbishops, 15 Bishops of named sees, 8 other Bishops, 5 masters of the Church, 10 Abbots, 7 named archpriests and Canons and other priests, [accordingly a large representative body]. The answers which they gave to the Roman enquiries about their faith are,

1 Objection. "That some ancient masters of the Armenians said and taught, that the Holy Spirit proceedeth from the Son as also from the Father."

Ans. "This is true, for although we have exceeding little on this subject, yet in some places in our books is found the Procession of the Spirit from the Son as from the Father, as in the Prayer of Pentecost, which is read in common in every year in the whole Church of the Armenians, and the

[n] I follow the translation of Malan (MS. Letter). Galanus has "ab utriusque essentia existentem." Malan cites Mich. Tchamtcheans Armenian History [ii. 685, 686.] "a standard work, though by a Mechitarist." See also Malan's Life of S. Gregory the Illuminator.

[o] Published by Martene and Durand from a MS. of the Royal Library at Paris (Vet. Mon. T. vii. p. 310), then reprinted in the SS. Concil. Collectio nova, ed. Mansi iii. 443 sqq. then in Mansi Conc. xxv. 1185 sqq.   [p] Mansi Ib. p. 444.

prayer says thus, 'Who art, O Lord, Lord of hosts and Very God, fountain of life, and in Thee, proceeding inscrutably from the Father and the Son, operating marvellous things, the Holy Spirit.' And S. Cyril saith, 'It is necessary to confess that the Spirit is of the Essence of the Son; for, as He is from Him according to Essence, so being sent from Him to creatures, He worketh renewal,' and the like."

3 Objection. "And if at times it is found in their books, that the Holy Spirit proceedeth from the Son, they understand this Procession of His temporal Procession to sanctify the creature, not of His eternal Procession, whereby in Personal Being He proceedeth eternally from the Father and the Son."

Ans. "This too is not true: for when in our books, the Holy Ghost is spoken of as proceeding from the Father and the Son, this is either spiritually or as a Person. Where the words do not relate or point to creatures, but to the Persons of the Father and the Son, there we understand it of the Eternal Procession, as in the prayer above; but when the Holy Spirit is given or sent by the Son to creatures to work renewal and to sanctify them, then we understand it of His temporal Procession. Therefore they do not say well."

But only such Armenians, as were united to Rome, had it in the Creed, as they would have had it, had they learned the doctrine from Rome. They had also a native Creed, framed in part for their own wants. This appears from a fourth objection,

Objection. "Also that the Armenians pronounce the article of faith inserted in the Creed thus, 'I believe in the Holy Ghost, Uncreated and Perfect, Who spake in the law and the prophets and the Gospels, and descended in Jordan, and preached in the Apostles and dwelleth in the saints, making no mention that the Holy Spirit proceedeth from the Father, or from the Father and the Son."

Ans. "The holy fathers added 'Uncreated and Perfect,' against heretics, who said that the Spirit was created and imperfect. And as to the assertion, that they make no mention in the Creed, that the Holy Spirit proceedeth from the Father, nor from the Father and the Son, although this is found in some places from the defect of the Scribes or the negligence of Prelates, yet commonly there occurs in books and it is recited in the Creed of the Armenians, 'And in the Holy Spirit, Who proceedeth from the Father.'"

They add in contrast to this,

"And after the Church of the Armenians was united with the Roman Church, we say plainly and teach, that the Holy Spirit proceedeth from the Son as from the Father."

6 Objection. "But many of them deny that the Holy Spirit proceedeth from the Son. And if some believe this, yet they do not venture to say it plainly."

Ans. "We have never found that the Church of the Armenians was opposed to the Procession of the Holy Spirit from the Son, or that it did not dare confidently to teach it."

The declaration of Bishops from all Armenia shews, that the belief in the Procession of the Holy Ghost from the Son also continued to be part of the traditional belief embodied in their prayers. It is a statement of a simple fact, of which they could not but be cognizant, that a prayer, containing this doctrine, was used throughout the Armenias.

Other evidence has been alleged but not as yet verified [q]:

[q] "Boghos Dadian in a letter to Mgr. Sibour Archbishop of

In "the confession of faith of the orthodox Armenian Church [r]," or " the instruction in the Christian Faith according to the Orthodox Armenian Church of S. Gregory the Illuminator," mention is only made of the Procession from the Father. The exclusive word of the modern Greeks, "from the Father *alone*," is not used.

Dathevatsi, who, I am informed, is "[s] one of the greatest authorities in the Armenian Church," only denies that the Son is *the* Cause. The teaching most naturally expresses the belief of the old fathers, and of the West.

> "[t]Not, as some think, is the Son *the* Cause of the eructation or pouring forth of the Spirit. For the Father is the Cause of It and of the taking of It by

Paris, quoted also as from S. Gregory the Illuminator: 'The Father is of Himself, the Son is of the Father; the Holy Ghost is of Them and in Them,' and said, that 'The above formula was often prefixed by the Patriarchs of Armenia to their pastoral letters.' He quoted also from " S. Eliseus, in a passage preserved by the historian Vartan: 'The first Person is Begotten of none; the Second is Begotten from the First; the Third emanates and proceeds from the Second and the First, as the fruit issues from the tree and from the root.'" (Rev. C. G. Curtis letter to the Guardian dated Pera Jan. 28, 1873.) Mr. Malan tells me that neither exists in any known writing of S. Gregory or of S. Eliseus.

[r] "Instruction" translated from the Armenian by the Rev. S. C. Malan p. 13. "Confession &c. p. 256, 266-268. The Roman Armenians allege older authorities on their side, according to Mr. Malan p. 268 note. F. Neve's work, De l'invocation du S. Esprit dans la Liturgie Armenienne, does not seem to me to furnish any evidence except as to the Armenians united to the Church of Rome. [s] The Rev. S. C. Malan, MS. letter.

[t] Questions, p. 109 Arm. translated for me by the Rev. C. S. Malan, who refers to "Nerses of Lampron in his Comm. on the Armenian Liturgy, p. 250."

the Son: for the Holy Ghost issues from the Father and is taken [or received] by the Son."

One is even surprised to find in the Armenian Church the accuracy of the expression of our Western fathers, that God the Son receiveth all from the Father, and so that He is not the primary Cause of the Being of God the Holy Ghost, because He receiveth it from the Father.

Had I been writing a Theological treatise, there would have been much more to add, for which I must refer those, who wish to pursue the subject further, to the learned and careful work of F. Pétau, which has, to such an extent, supplied me with my material, both now and heretofore. But I have not been writing on this special subject of Theology, the Being of Almighty God, in His awful Majesty. I have simply been addressing myself to a practical subject, which pressed upon us. When we heard rumours of the good disposition of Greek authorities towards the English Church, it came to us in this simple form; the Greeks " cannot refuse our Communion, on the ground that we use the self-same language, which great fathers of their own used." With this view, after the Archbishop of Syra had visited England, and the Archbishop of Chios had written his remarkable peacemaking essays, some of us transmitted to the authorities at Constantinople, extracts from the writings of their great father, S. Cyril of Alexandria, unmistakeable in their teaching and guaranteed from any supposition, that they could have been tampered with by Latins, because, existing in Syriac translations or in MSS. in their own possession, they were out of the reach of

Westerns. But we were only private unauthorised individuals; and naturally, our communication (if even it was received), remained unnoticed. The Bonn conference opened fresh difficulties. For instead of addressing itself to the only real point at issue, whether our Western language has not (as has often been virtually acknowledged, and as was formally stated at Florence) precisely the same meaning as that which prevailed in Greece, it seemed good to those present there, to soothe Greek prejudices upon a point of etiquette, how our Western formula came into our Western translation of a Greek Creed, received by the Council of Chalcedon. This, if our Western formula represents a truth, was, of course, utterly indifferent, so long as no one attempted to impose it on the East. And the Easterns, with their claim of autonomy and their reverence for antiquity, could not legitimately interfere with our devotions of at least 1200 years. But prejudices have very often more weight than the real issue. And the prejudices were popularly augmented by the imputation of "arbitrariness," "interpolation," supposed "aggression" of some king or Pope, which last is in itself by many Englishmen regarded as decisive against any thing, in which a Bishop of Rome happens to have been concerned. As all these suppositions were directly contrary to the truth, I hoped that it might diminish prejudice to point out their baselessness.

The real point at issue between the Eastern and Western Church on the Procession, lies within a narrow compass. If the Greeks come to understand our Western term[u], all difference disappears. We

[u] See ab. pp. 106, 107.

impute no heresy to them, hoping that they adhere to the faith of their old fathers. At one time forefathers of theirs wished, in the strife, to make the breach as wide as they could. Their later formula that "the Holy Ghost proceedeth out of the Father *alone*," is (as some of their own writers have pointed out) as much "an addition" as that for which they blame us, "proceedeth from the Father and the Son [v]." Yet even that later formula is only apparently contradictory to our's, if, by it, they mean only to assert that God the Father is the Original Head of the Coeternal Trinity. The only difference between us would arise, if they should deny an eternal relation between God the Son and God the Holy Ghost; that God the Holy Ghost is Third, *not* in time, but in the Order of the Divine Existence, Existing eternally from the Father and the Son, as One [w].

This Eternal relation is manifestly laid down in the Order revealed by our Lord in the form, in which He directed His own to be baptised. For since the order is not of the superiority of the One to the Other, it must be only, as S. Basil said [x], of the mode of existence. This is the order which was engrafted upon the doxologies of the Universal Church: this lies in all our Creeds, and is written in the hearts of all Christians. The inverse order is used by S. Paul [y], yet in exactly the same mean-

[v] In another way, their Patriarch, John Beccus, came to see that since it was said by the fathers, that "the Spirit proceeded from the Father *through* the Son, speaking of the Theology of the Spirit" [i.e. of His Being as God], the Greek " fathers too made an addition." Pachymeres ii. p. 27 Bonn.   [w] See S. Aug. above p. 145.

[x] Above, p. 108, 109.   [y] 1 Cor. xii. 4-6.

ing. He mentions first the Holy Spirit; then the Son; then the Father. "But we must not think," says S. Basil[z], "that the order is wholly reversed. For he [S. Paul] began from the relation to us. Since we, who receive the gifts, first come in contact with Him Who distributeth them; then we have in mind Him, Who sent; then we carry up our thoughts to the Fountain and Cause of all good."

It lies also in that title of Holy Scripture which the Greeks too acknowledge and cannot but acknowledge, that the Holy Ghost is "the Spirit of the Son." For Holy Scripture speaks of the One belonging to the Other, only by reason of the eternal relation, as coeternally existing from Him. In that absolute Unity and Coequality of the All-Holy Trinity, One Person cannot be said to appertain to Another, except as existing eternally from Him. But the Spirit is said to be "the Spirit of the Son;" the Son is nowhere said to be " of the Spirit" but "of the Father" only. Again, it belongs to the exactness of the saying, "All which the Father hath, is Mine," "All Mine are Thine and Thine are Mine," as also to the Unity of God, that all of the Father should belong to the Son, save being the Father, and so the being with the Father the Source of the Being of the Holy Spirit. It lies also in those words of His, "He shall receive of Mine," which the fathers so often identify with those, "Who proceedeth from the Father." For the Holy Ghost could not take from the Son any thing which He had not by His Very Being, else He would not be One with Him. Greek fathers also interpreted in

---

[z] de Sp. S. c. 16. Pet. vii. 6-3.

the same way S. Paul's words, "Whom He knew, He also did predestinate to be conformed to the Image of His Son;" whence even S. John of Damascus says (as he was quoted at Bonn) "the Holy Ghost is the Image of the Son;" and, if this be the right interpretation, it also would imply a special relation of the Spirit to the Son, as of the Son to the Father. This belief must have been the more prominent in the mind of great Greek Fathers, since they saw this relation, where our modern minds would not commonly perceive it.

There must have been some reason in the mind of God, why our Lord, while on earth, referred all things to the Father. His Life, His Will, His doctrine, His mighty works, were, He said, "My Father's." To have declared Himself plainly to be Almighty God might have ended His mission prematurely; as in due time it closed it. But He said "Who proceedeth from the Father:" He did not say, "Who proceedeth from the Father Alone." He left that teaching, like all the rest, to be filled up by that Holy Spirit, Who declared Himself by His Apostles to be "the Spirit of the Son," to be, i.e., to have His Being from Him.

In conclusion, for myself, I thank God for this delay of the Bonn Conference, under the expectation of which I began this letter to you. Desiring, as earnestly as any, the healthful filling up of any of the cracks which outwardly separate what, where there is no heresy, I hope, down deep below, is one, and especially with the ancient Eastern Church, I am sure that untimely haste will only make the rent worse, or make fresh rents. Cleaving, as the Greek Church desires to do, to the faith of their fathers, I trust that they will discover on reflection that those among them, who hold only a temporal Procession of God the Holy Ghost from the Father and the Son together to their creatures [a], do in fact destroy the eternal relation of the Third Person of the Adorable Trinity to the Second, and conceive of God as existing otherwise than He has revealed

[a] Bessarion, in a declaration appended to his "Oratio dogmatica" at the Council of Florence (Conc. T. 18. 465. Col.) says, that "the Greeks have four evasions of the force of the word διὰ used by their great fathers: i) that the words, with which it is used, signify only the distribution of His graces and gifts to us, and His temporal mission into the world, which they grant to be through the Son. ii) Because Father and Son are relative names, and that one of two relatives cannot be spoken of, without the other being understood; therefore in saying 'from the Father' it is necessary to name the Son, on account of the force of the relation. iii) They say that the Consubstantiality of the Father and the Son is the reason that the Spirit is said to proceed from the Father through the Son; for since the Father and the Son are of the same Substance, when it is said, "from the Father," it must needs also be said, "from the Son." iv.) Because sometimes, but very rarely and among poets, (who, for the metre, used words metaphorically and inaccurately) they have found the preposition *through* sometimes to have the same sense as *with*, they say that the Holy Spirit is therefore said to proceed from the Father *through* the Son, because He proceeds from the Father together *with* the Son." These explanations are manifestly alternative, excluding one another. i.) only takes the *through* in a natural sense, yet alone relates to time; the rest presuppose that the *through* relates to the Eternal Procession; but oddly enough, assume that *through* does not mean *through*; iv.) boldly says that *through* means *with*. They are manifestly the shifts of persons evading the Faith expressed by their forefathers by the word. Bessarion shews their inapplicability to the passages of the fathers, which they were to explain away. Orat. dogm. c. 6. Conc. T. 18. 422. sqq.

Himself. It is startling to hear S. Epiphanius or S. Athanasius deny that the Holy Spirit is "the Brother of the Son;" it shocks us to have to deny, as to God, a relation analogous to one of our human relations, which God has not revealed to us of Himself. But it is, in our human words, what the denial of the eternal Procession of the Holy Ghost "from" or "through the Son" comes to. For God the Son and God the Holy Ghost issued forth from the Father's Being, as the Source and Original of Each. If then the Holy Ghost had not (which these deny) proceeded eternally "through the Son," but had proceeded from the Father independently of the Son, they had had to each other that relation which in our human likeness had been that of brothers.

It would also much impair our idea of the Unity of God in the Adorable Trinity, did we conceive of Two of the Persons as having no relation to one another, except an independent relation to the One Father. The truth of the mutual Inexistence [b] of the Three Blessed Persons, which our Lord reveals to us by the words, "I am in the Father and the Father in Me," "The Father Who abideth in Me," facilitates to us the conception of the simple Unity of God in the All-Holy Trinity. The doctrine excludes Arianism on the one side, and Sabellianism on the other; "neither confounding the Persons, nor dividing the Substance." The Fathers had most occasion to dwell upon this against the Arians. In our human mode of existence, the father is external to the son, and the breath from the breather. In

[b] περιχώρησις. See Petav. de Trin. iv. 16. *per totum*, Dr. Newman, notes on S. Athanasius against the Arians, Oxf. Tr. *passim*.

God, all is one within Himself, in the absolute unity and simplicity of His Being.

"How," asks S. Cyril[c], "could God be conceived as being One, if each Person withdrew into an entire individuality, and, wholly removed from the essential union and mutual relation, were called God?"

"[d] In no way can there be imagined any division or separation, so that the Son could be conceived of without the Father, or the Spirit be disjoined from the Son.—But in Them is apprehended a certain at once communion and disjunction beyond words or thought." "[e] They are united, not so as to be confused, but as to cohere together; and they have In-existence in each other, without any commingling or confusion; nor are they parted from one another, or divided in essence, according to the division of Arius. But to speak concisely, Deity is, in Separates Inseparate[f].

"[g] In the Godhead we confess one Nature, but say that there are in truth three Persons, and we say, that all which is of nature and essence is simple, but we acknowledge the difference of Persons in these three properties only; the being Uncaused and Father; or caused and Son; or caused and Proceeding; but we know that they go not forth apart from Each other, and are inseparate and united, and inexist unconfusedly in Each other, and are united without confusion (for They are Three although they are united) and are, without division, distinct. For although Each exists by Himself, i. e., is perfectly a Person, and has His own property, i. e., His own separate mode of Being, yet they are united in Essence and natural properties, and by their not being

[c] See S. Cyril on S. John p. 53. Oxf. Tr.. [d] S. Basil Ep. 38 n. 4. Opp. iii. 118. Ben. [e] Damascene in Petav. iv. 16. 7.
[f] ἀμέριστος ἐν μεμερισμένοις. [g] Damasc. de fid. orth. iii. 5.

separated or going apart from the Person of the Father, both are and are called One God."

"By the natural unity," S. Fulgentius says[h], "the whole Father is in the Son and Holy Spirit, the whole Son is in the Father and Holy Spirit, the whole Holy Spirit also is in the Father and the Son. None of these is external to any one of them, for none precedeth another in eternity, or exceeds in magnitude, or overpasseth in power."

and Alcuin[i]:

" God by the immensity of His Nature filleth and containeth the whole creation, and thereby the Father filleth the whole, whatever is; the Son the whole; the Holy Spirit the whole. Wherefore also the Son and the Holy Spirit are by nature, One. The inseparable unity therefore of nature cannot have separable Persons. But this nature of Supreme Trinity and individual Unity, which Alone is whole everywhere, as it hath everywhere inseparable Unity of nature or operation, so it cannot receive separation of Persons."

This Inexistence of the Divine Persons, which our Divine Lord lays down in the words, " I am in the Father and the Father in Me," is essential to any intelligent conception of the Divine Unity. The absence of the belief in it has been at the root of every heresy as to the Holy Trinity. Apart from the " from " or " through," it is contained in every expression, that God the Holy Ghost is "in the Son" "is essentially Inexistent in Him," "is in Him and His own," " in Him by Nature."

In the order of the Divine existence, contained in the baptismal formula which our Lord prescribed to us, Father, Son, and Holy Ghost, the Father, as

[h] de fide ad Petr. c. l.   [i] de Trin. i. 14.

our Lord says, ever exists in the Son, Who eternally and unchangeably has His existence from Him in the Immensity of Godhead, and the Father and the Son, being One, ever inexist in the Holy Spirit, Who is breathed forth from Both. Take away this belief, and the Inexistence is gone. Such introduce division into the Godhead, a sort of duality of existence, the Father being supposed ever to produce the Son by Generation, the Holy Ghost by Procession, but God the Son and God the Holy Ghost having no relation to one another.

The loss of the " and the Son" would to our untheological practical English mind involve the loss of the doctrine of the Trinity.

The Western statement of the Procession of the Holy Ghost "from the Father and the Son" was not, as far as we know, framed as a corrective of any heretical teaching; but it has, in the good Providence of God, been a great preservative against heresy, which would not have been guarded against by the Greek formula, " through the Son." For although this, in the language of the Greek fathers, expressed the same doctrine, yet it admitted also of a meaning, compatible with a denial of the Faith, as contained in the Baptismal formula, given us by our Lord. The thirst for visible unity has directed itself the more towards the Greek Church, since the Roman Church has shut against us what seemed to be a half-open door. But therewith there has, among some, seemed to be a rising impatience of the " Filioque," as though it were *the* hindrance to an union with the Eastern Church. Middle-age Greek writers have surmised that the ground of the prolonged

schism was not the doctrine, but "the thrones [k],"
Constantinople wishing to have an eminence over the
other Eastern Patriarchates, which did not belong to
it; Rome claiming an authority over Constantinople
and the East, which it did not claim in primitive
times. There seemed then the more hope, that
since *this* question did not lie between Greece and
ourselves, they could not, if they would look into the
question, except against our retaining the expression
of the faith, which we have in common with their
own fathers. Whether this will be so, He alone
knoweth Who disposeth the hearts of men. One
thing is certain, that we must not, in a desire for a
premature union, abandon the expression of our
faith for at least 1200 years. However the faith
may be maintained by tradition in the East, but,
in fact certainly is, more or less widely, *not* maintained there [1], we, by parting with our inherited ex-

[k] e. g. "Although the schism is said to have been renewed
under Sergius, I know not for what reason; but I think, on account of the sees." Nicetas Nicænus in Le Quien p. xii. The
ground of the failure of attempts at re-union seems to have been
the subjection to Rome involved. See also "one of their able and
moderate writers, Elias Meniates, Bishop of Zerniza, towards the
end of the 17th cent., Lapis offensionis, L. ii. c. 1. quoted by
M. Trevern, Discussion Amicale, T. i. p. 231," in Dr. Pusey's
Eirenicon I. p. 63.

[1] On the belief formerly for above 200 years from Cerularius,
see ab. p. 94; on the evasions at the time of the Council of Florence see ab. p. 175. For the present, I would hope that the
cases, which I know of, of the denial of the eternal Procession
may be balanced by others, who believe it; any how, that such
may come to a full belief. The Greeks hold S. John Damascene
to represent the fathers before him: they esteem his authority
highly: let them ascertain for themselves his real meaning; they
will not be removed, except in language, from the West.

pression of it, should forfeit the belief itself, and become misbelievers in our God.

You will receive in your love this my last contribution, in this direction, to a future which I shall not see. It was touching to see the confidence, which their old Patriarch John Beccus, who suffered so much in the attempt to soften the prejudices of the Greeks and to promote union, had in the distant future. Although the present did not receive what he undertook, "[m]he trusted to those of a later generation." *We* have not the difficulties which kept Greece and Rome out of communion with each other. We have no requirements to make of them; we have only to ask them to tolerate our expression of our common faith which (we cannot insist too often) was the expression of great fathers of their own also. But our Lord laid it down as a great rule of the kingdom of God, "One soweth and another reapeth." We sow the seed, trusting that God may give the increase in a later generation. I have been mainly employed in removing hindrances which overlay it. But the forceful words of their own fathers which I have embodied will, I trust, speak to the hearts of some of our Eastern friends, and God, in Whose Hand alone are the hearts of His creatures, will "turn the hearts of the children to the fathers," and give us peace.

May God continue to prosper and bless all which you would do for Him and His Glory.

Your most affectionate friend,

JULY, 1876.   E. B. PUSEY.

[m] πιστεύων τοῖς ὀψιγόνοις in Pachymeres ii. 28.

NOTE I.

The Bonn Propositions with amendments suggested to some of them.

Preliminary Resolutions.

I. "We agree together in receiving the Œcumenical Symbola, and the doctrinal decisions of the ancient Undivided Church."

II. "We agree together in acknowledging that the addition of the *Filioque* to the Creed *did not take place in an ecclesiastically regular manner.*"

Amendment suggested;

II. "*We agree together in acknowledging that the addition of the Filioque in the Latin copies of the Niceno-Constantinopolitan Creed, having come in under a wrong impression, that it was part of the Creed settled at the Qouncil of Constantinople, and not having itself the authority of any General Council, ought never to have been enforced upon the Greek Church* [a].*"*

III. "We acknowledge on all sides the representation of the doctrine of the Holy Ghost as it is set forth by the Fathers of the Undivided Church."

IV. "We reject every proposition and every mode of expression, in which in any way the acknowledgment of two Principles or ἀρχαὶ or αἰτίαι in the Trinity *may be* contained."

Proposed amendment [b];

"*is* contained,"

or, more simply,

"*We deny the supposition of two Principles in the Trinity, as contrary to our belief in the Unity of God.*"

[a] See Letter p. 33-93.   [b] See ab. p. 99.

Then in regard to the doctrine itself, for
"*On the Procession of the Holy Ghost.*

"We accept *the teaching of S. John of Damascus*[c] respecting the Holy Ghost, as the same is expressed in the following paragraphs, in the sense of the teaching of the *ancient undivided Church:*"

Amendment suggested;
"*We accept the following propositions as agreeable to the teaching of the undivided Church.*"

Bonn doctrinal propositions;

1. "The Holy Ghost goeth forth out of the Father (ἐκ τοῦ πατρός) as the Beginning (ἀρχή), the Cause (αἰτία), the Source (πηγή), of the Godhead."

2. "The Holy Ghost goeth not forth out of the Son (ἐκ τοῦ υἱοῦ), because there is in the Godhead but one Beginning (ἀρχή) one Cause (αἰτία) through which all that is in the Godhead is produced."

Proposed amendment to Prop. 2[d].

2. "The Holy Ghost goes not forth out of the Son (ἐκ τοῦ υἱοῦ) *as a distinct Source of Being,* because there is in the Godhead but one Beginning (ἀρχή) one Cause (αἰτία)."

Or more briefly;

2. "*The Holy Ghost goes not forth out of the Son as a Beginning or Primary Cause.*"

Bonn Prop. 3.

"The Holy Ghost goes forth out of the Father through the Son."

Amendment
(to prevent ambiguity, being contained in the context of two of the passages of S. John of Damascus quoted[e])

3. "*The Holy Ghost goes forth out of the Father through the Son eternally.*"

[c] See ab. pp. 96, 97.   [d] See ab. p. 98.
[e] See ab. pp. 99, 100.

And in place of the three last, viz.

4. "The Holy Ghost is the image of the Son, Who is the image of the Father, going forth out of the Father and existing in the Son, as the force beaming forth from Him."

5. "The Holy Ghost is the personal production out of the Father, belonging to the Son, but not out of the Son, because He is the Spirit of the mouth of the Godhead, which speaks forth the word."

6. "The Holy Ghost forms the mediation between the Father and the Son, and is bound together to the Father through the Son."

Amendment

4. "*The Holy Ghost proceedeth from the Father and the Son together, since they are essentially One, but principially from the Father* [f]."

[f] See ab. pp. 107-141.

NOTE II.

Contemporary account of the direction of the Emperor Justin II. to sing the Creed of Constantinople in the East, shortly before it was enjoined by the 3rd Council of Toledo [a].

John, Abbot of Biclaro [Vallis claræ] "[b] had studied at Constantinople, for 17 years, had returned to Spain under the Arian king Leuvigild, had been banished by him to Barcino [Barcelona]," was recalled from banishment by king Recarede and made Bishop of Girone A.D. 592 [c]. His Chronicle was a supplement to that of Victor of Tunis from A. D. 566 to 590, i.e. from the 1st of the younger Justin to the 8th of the Emperor Maurice [d]. The author was then a contemporary. But he says,

[a] See ab. p. 49. [b] Isid. Hisp. de virr. ill. c. 31.
[c] Nic. Ant. Bibl. vet. Hisp. iv. 5. T. i. p. 227. in Gall. Proleg. T. xii. c. 17. [d] Gallandi l. c. n. 2.

"ᵉ The younger Justin in the 1st year of his reign, annulled what had been devised against the Council of Chalcedon, and introduced the Creed of the 150 holy fathers, gathered at Constantinople, and laudably received in the Council of Chalcedon, to be sung by the people in every Catholic Church, before the Lord's prayer be said."

ᵉ Joann. Biclar. Chron. in Gall. Bibl. Patr. xii. 365. Le Q.

NOTE III.

Corrections of some statements of Bishop Pearson about the insertion of the Filioque in our Western use of the Creed.

As the statements and authority of our good and learned Bishop Pearson have been employed so widely and accepted as certain, it seemed to be even reverent to his great name, and to belong to our pious affection for him, to correct them in points, in which he acquiesced in a popular opinion which was gravely inaccurate.

Bishop Pearson believed too readily the statement of Photius, which Photius himself contradicted ᵃ, that Pope Nicolas I. inserted the *Filioque* into the Creed. Nor was he acquainted with the entire innocency and dutifulness to the Council of Constantinople, in which the clause first came into our Western version of the Creed. In his account, these inaccurate statements are involved: 1) That the Constantinopolitan Creed was at once " received by the whole Church of God." [It was not received for 71 years ᵇ.] 2) That it was "added by the next General Council of Ephesus, that it should not be lawful to make any addition to it." [The Council of Ephesus did not receive the Constantinopolitan Creed itself, but only the original Creed of Nice. If then it had forbidden any *true* " explanations ᶜ " of the Nicene, it would have condemned the Constantinopolitan Creed, which contained such explanations]. 3)"Notwithstanding, the question being agitated in the West,

ᵃ See ab. p. 67.   ᵇ Ib. p. 36-42.   ᶜ Ib. p. 76-92.

Utrum Spiritus Sanctus, sicut procedit a Patre, ita et procedat a Filio, and it being concluded in the affirmative, they did not only declare the doctrine to be true, but also added the same to the Constantinopolitan Creed and sang it publicly in their liturgy." Bishop Pearson is not to be blamed for not having read the Acts of the third Council of Toledo. But at the time of that Council, a) there was no *question* in the West about the Procession of the Holy Ghost. All Westerns believed and confessed (as we do), that He proceeded from the Father and the Son. b) The Westerns did not "declare the doctrine to be true;" there was no occasion to declare, what had never been questioned. c) They did not "add the statement" to the Constantinopolitan Creed, but received the Creed with the addition, fully believing it to be the Creed of Constantinople [d].

After giving the first opinion of Leo III. that it would be better to remove the *Filioque*, Bp. P. omits his final acquiescence in the suggestion of the Legates, that this would shake men's faith, and that he advised only the gradual disuse of chanting it in the royal Chapel [e]. 4) "The following Popes" [after Leo III.] "more in love with their own authority, than desirous of the peace and unity of the Church, admitted the addition *Filioque*. This was first done in the time and by the power of Pope Nicolaus the first, who by the activity of Photius was condemned for it." Photius only heard this on rumour, and three times asserted the contrary. There is no proof that it was ever formally received by any Council or any Pope before the 2nd General Council of Lyons, at which Greek Bishops were present [f]. Photius was at this time not legitimate Patriarch of Constantinople; Ignatius, the rightful Patriarch, was restored immediately afterwards by Basilius Macedo, whose coronation (murderer though he was) Photius had celebrated and whom he had communicated [g]. The so-called Synod in which Photius took upon him to depose Nicolaus, was signed only by

[d] See ab. pp. 46-49.   [e] Ib. pp. 65, 66.
[f] Ib. pp. 14-16.   [g] Photius Ep. 97. p. 136. ed. Montac.

21 Bishops, to which Photius added 1000 forged signatures [h]. The Imperial Embassador affirmed on oath, that the signature of Basil was forged, and that of the Emperor Michael was obtained from him, when very drunk at night, by Photius [i].

5. "After Photius was restored again, in the 8th General Council as the Greeks call it, it was declared that the addition of the *Filioque* made in the Creed should be taken away."

What some Greeks call the 8th General Council (others acknowledge *seven* only [j], counting the Council of Florence the *eighth* [k],) was a mere magnifying of Photius, by whom it was held after the death of Ignatius. In this his agents took advantage of the Roman legates' ignorance of Greek to impose upon them [l]. After the Synod was completed and signed, the *Greek* acts contain two more, whose genuineness is questioned [m]. In the last of these, it is declared, with the approbation, it is said, of the Roman legates, that "[n] the spiritual presidency of the whole world was given to Photius." It is, of course, absolutely incredible that the

[h] Anastasius in his preface to the Latin version of the Acts of the 8th. (General) Council. Conc. x. 474. Col.

[i] Adriani Vita by Continuator of Anastas. Conc. x. 394. Col.

[j] Pagi 869 n. 16.   [k] Abraham of Crete so entitled it in his edition and Clement vii adopted the title in his Bull sanctioning the edition.   [l] Neander iv. 434 admits this.

[m] Assem. Bibl. jur. orient. T. i. pp. 222. 226. They were held, or alleged to be held, not in the Church but in the Imperial Palace Chrysotriklinium.

[n] Procopius said, "Such ought he in truth to be, who has received the superintendence of the whole world after the pattern of the Chief Shepherd, Christ our God, which also the blessed Paul sketched out when he said, 'we having a high-priest who hath passed into the heavens.' For my speech may advance even so far, since the Scripture called those gods who live according to grace." "The most holy legates of the elder Rome said, 'True is it which thou hast spoken; for we who live at the ends of the earth know this.'" Act. vii. fin. Conc. xi. 497. Col.

Roman legates could have approved of this, if they understood what it meant. But they were the only representatives of the West; without them it would be a Greek Council only.

In the other Session, Mark of Ephesus must have been mistaken in affirming (as he did at Florence) that "[o] it was decreed, that the addition in the Creed should be wholly taken away." For, according to Photius himself, his legate had found the Creed *preserved* unchanged among the Romans [p]. What was done, if *this* session was genuine, was, that the Creed was recited without the Filioque, and all additions prohibited in regard to newly-converted nations, in the strong terms which Photius would use, probably in reference to his old charge about the Bulgarians.

6. "After this, the same complaint was continued [rather renewed after 123 years] by Michael Cerularius."

This was an after-thought of Cerularius to justify the schism: at first he said that the faith in the Holy Trinity was the same, and that the Latins stumbled in only one thing, the use of unleavened bread in the Holy Eucharist [q].

With regard to Bishop Pearson's opinion that the schism was thus occasioned, Greek authorities too have been of opinion, that it was "on account of the sees [r]." With regard to the repeated statements, that a General Council had prohibited all addition and that the Latins relied on the authority of the Pope to alter any thing; the meaning of the Canon of Ephesus was cleared by the Council of Chalcedon and others [s]; and it has been shewn that the last place in the West, in which the innocently enlarged Creed was received, was Rome [t].

[o] Quoted by Bishop Pearson l. c.
[p] See ab. p. 68.   [q] Ab. p. 69.   [r] Ab. p. 180.
[s] Ab. p. 75-93.   [t] Ab. p. 66.

www.ingramcontent.com/pod-product-compliance
Lightning Source LLC
Chambersburg PA
CBHW032129160426
43197CB00008B/574